Oxford
Primary
Science
Dictionary

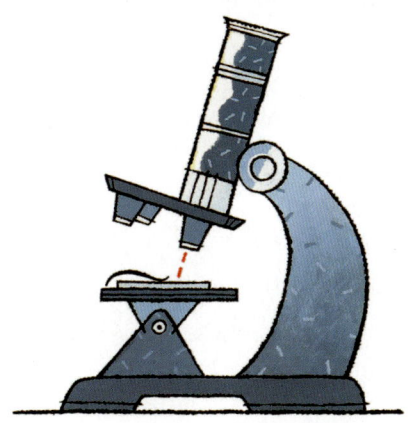

Compiled by Graham Peacock

OXFORD
UNIVERSITY PRESS

OXFORD
UNIVERSITY PRESS

Great Clarendon Street, Oxford OX2 6DP

Oxford University Press is a department of the University of Oxford.
It furthers the University's objective of excellence in research, scholarship,
and education by publishing worldwide in

Oxford   New York

Auckland   Cape Town   Dar es Salaam   Hong Kong   Karachi
Kuala Lumpur   Madrid   Melbourne   Mexico City   Nairobi
New Delhi   Shanghai   Taipei   Toronto

With offices in

Argentina   Austria   Brazil   Chile   Czech Republic   France   Greece
Guatemala   Hungary   Italy   Japan   Poland   Portugal   Singapore
South Korea   Switzerland   Thailand   Turkey   Ukraine   Vietnam

Oxford is a registered trade mark of Oxford University Press
in the UK and in certain other countries

British Library Cataloguing in Publication Data

Data available

ISBN 978 0 19 911687 4 (paperback)
3 5 7 9 10 8 6 4
ISBN 978 0 19 911686 7 (hardback)
1 3 5 7 9 10 8 6 4 2
ISBN 978 0 19 576557 1 (S.A. edition)
1 3 5 7 9 10 8 6 4 2

Printed in Malaysia by Imago

Paper used in the production of this book is a natural, recyclable
product made from wood grown in sustainable forests. The
manufacturing process conforms to the environmental regulations
of the country of origin.

www.schooldictionaries.co.uk

Contents

Introduction

The Oxford Primary Science Dictionary contains over 600 words in alphabetical order, each with an easy-to-understand meaning. It is an ideal way to build children's specific subject vocabulary.

The words in the Oxford Primary Science Dictionary are drawn from the words used in primary school science teaching, along with scientific words that are in common everyday use. Where a word has several meanings, all of them are given.

The main features of the A-Z pages are:

captions show the word in context and give further information ⟶

short definition (meaning) ⟶

headword ⟶

accurate diagram to help clarify definition ⟶

page number ⟶

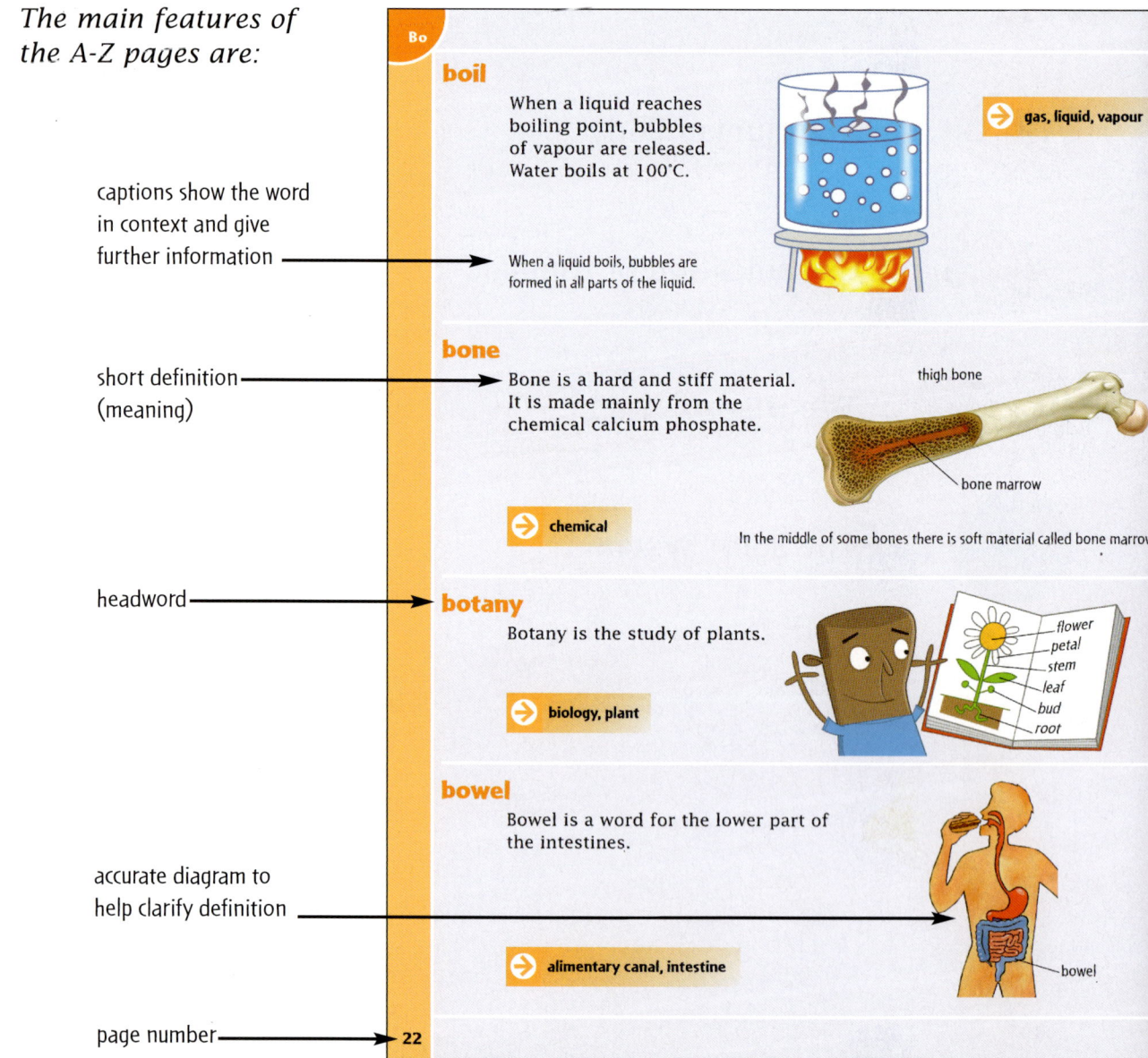

Bo

boil

When a liquid reaches boiling point, bubbles of vapour are released. Water boils at 100°C.

→ gas, liquid, vapour

When a liquid boils, bubbles are formed in all parts of the liquid.

bone

Bone is a hard and stiff material. It is made mainly from the chemical calcium phosphate.

→ chemical

thigh bone

bone marrow

In the middle of some bones there is soft material called bone marrow.

botany

Botany is the study of plants.

→ biology, plant

flower
petal
stem
leaf
bud
root

bowel

Bowel is a word for the lower part of the intestines.

→ alimentary canal, intestine

bowel

22

4

Detailed, accurate pictures and diagrams help make the meanings of entries clear. Explanatory captions give further examples of how the word is used.

A special 'link' word feature connects the entries in the dictionary. These are words that are also in the dictionary, which extend the meaning of the original word. The use of link words helps to encourage an understanding that many scientific ideas are connected. At the end of the book there are useful lists giving apparatus, information on the human body, classification, the history of life and the Solar System. There is also a full index to make finding words easy.

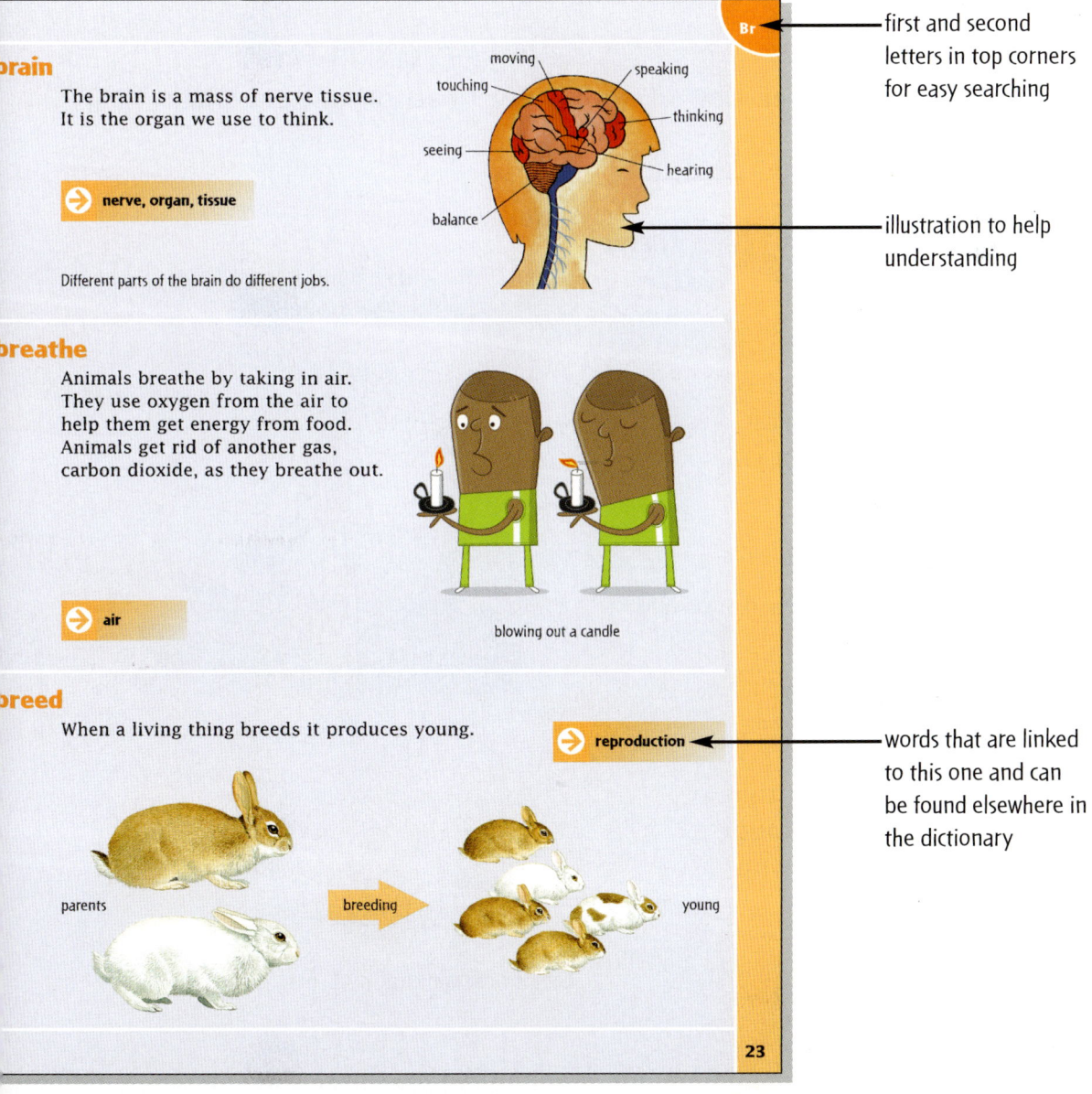

Br — first and second letters in top corners for easy searching

brain

The brain is a mass of nerve tissue. It is the organ we use to think.

→ **nerve, organ, tissue**

moving
touching
speaking
thinking
seeing
hearing
balance

Different parts of the brain do different jobs.

— illustration to help understanding

breathe

Animals breathe by taking in air. They use oxygen from the air to help them get energy from food. Animals get rid of another gas, carbon dioxide, as they breathe out.

→ **air**

blowing out a candle

breed

When a living thing breeds it produces young.

→ **reproduction**

— words that are linked to this one and can be found elsewhere in the dictionary

parents
breeding
young

23

abdomen

The abdomen is the stomach of an animal. It also contains the digestive organs (gut). Indigestion is an abdominal pain.

 gut, insect, intestine

abdomen

An insect's abdomen is at the end of its body.

absorb

Towels absorb water. Cotton wool is a very absorbent material.

The kitchen towel absorbs liquid, but the table top doesn't.

accelerate

When an object accelerates it goes faster and faster.

A rocket accelerates away from the launch pad.

acid

Acids are chemicals that have a sour taste. Plaque on teeth produces acid, which attacks tooth enamel.

 alkali, chemical, decay

Lemons contain citric acid.

acid rain

Acid rain is a kind of pollution. It is caused by certain gases which come from the chimneys of factories and power stations, and from the engines of cars and other vehicles.

waste gases mix with water in clouds

acids are formed

waste gases

acid falls as rain

adapted

Animals and plants are adapted to their environment. Their bodies are suited to the way they live.

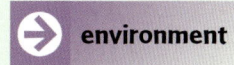
environment

An anteater's long nose and sticky tongue are adapted for poking into anthills and licking up ants.

addict

An addict is someone who has a habit they can't give up.

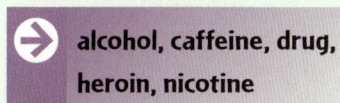
alcohol, caffeine, drug, heroin, nicotine

KICK YOUR ADDICTION!

ALCOHOLICS ARE ADDICTED TO DRINK!

DON'T MESS WITH DRUGS
YOU MAY BECOME ADDICTED!

aerobic

Aerobic exercise makes you breathe deeply. It means there is a good supply of oxygen to the muscles.

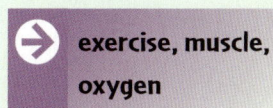
exercise, muscle, oxygen

aerodynamic

When an object is aerodynamic it slips through the air easily.

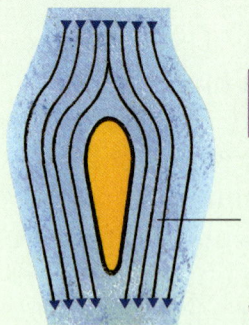

unsteady air flow

object not aerodynamic

object aerodynamic

smooth air flow

→ air, air resistance

Wind tunnels are used to test the air resistance of vehicles.

AIDS

AIDS is a disease that can be caught during sexual intercourse. It is caused by a virus called HIV. HIV weakens the body and this lets in many other infections.

→ condom, disease, germ, infect, sexual intercourse, virus

This is a magnified view of an HIV virus, cutaway to show the inside.

air

Air is the gas that we breathe.

→ atmosphere

Air is a mixture of different gases, mostly nitrogen and oxygen.

oxygen

nitrogen

argon

other gases

carbon dioxide

air resistance

Air resistance is the force that slows down objects that move through the air.

→ aerodynamic, parachute

A skydiver falls fast until he opens his parachute. Then air resistance on the parachute slows him down.

alcohol

Alcohol is a liquid that is part of many drinks. The alcohol in beer and wine can make people drunk.

It is illegal to sell alcohol to people under 18 years old.

algae

Algae are simple green plants that do not have roots. Some kinds form the green slime on paths and in ponds.

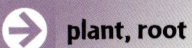

plant, root

Seaweeds are algae that live in the sea.

alien

1. Aliens are animals or plants that are living out of their usual habitat. The opposite of alien is indigenous.

2. Living things from another planet are aliens.

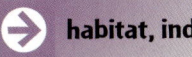

habitat, indigenous

This giraffe is a very long way from its usual habitat.

alimentary canal

The long tube from mouth to anus is called the alimentary canal.

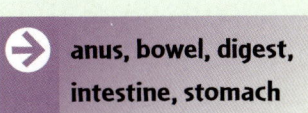

anus, bowel, digest, intestine, stomach

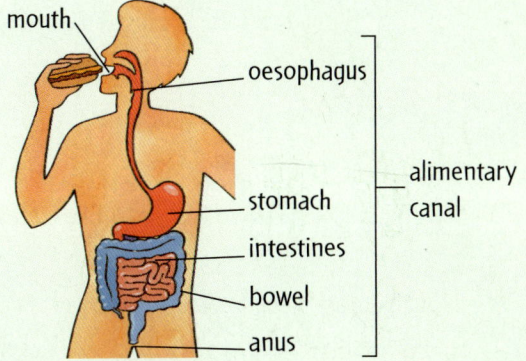

mouth
oesophagus
stomach
intestines
bowel
anus
alimentary canal

alive

Living things are alive. They can grow, breathe, reproduce, move, feed, and excrete waste material. The opposite of alive is dead.

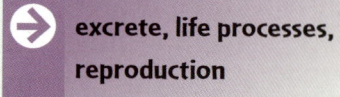
excrete, life processes, reproduction

reproducing   moving   feeding   excreting

alkali

Alkalis are the chemical opposites of acids.

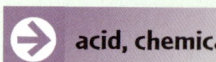
acid, chemical

Strong alkalis like bleach are dangerous.

allergy

An allergy is when the body reacts badly to a substance. Allergies often produce a skin rash or cause sneezing.

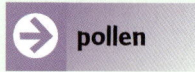
pollen

Hay fever is caused by an allergy to pollen.

alloy

A mixture of two metals is called an alloy.

metal

Trumpets are made of brass, an alloy of copper and zinc.

aluminium

Aluminium is a light-weight, silvery, non-magnetic metal that is used to make many things.

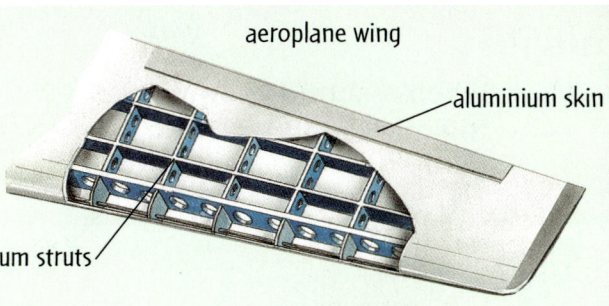

aeroplane wing

aluminium skin

aluminium struts

Aeroplanes are made from aluminium because it is light and strong.

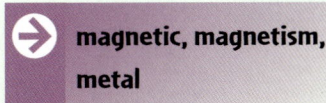
→ magnetic, magnetism, metal

ammonite

Ammonites are extinct animals that lived in the sea at the time of the dinosaurs.

→ fossil, dinosaur

Ammonites are found as fossils in rocks.

amp

Amps are units for measuring the flow of electric current.

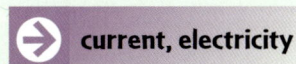
→ current, electricity

Plugs for heaters are fitted with 13-amp fuses while lights have 3-amp fuses.

amphibian

Frogs, newts, and toads are all amphibians. They start as eggs in water and breathe through gills. Later they develop lungs and live on land and in water.

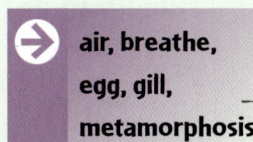
→ air, breathe, egg, gill, metamorphosis

tadpole

back legs grow

front legs grow

adult frog

Amphibians begin life as tadpoles.

amplify

When a sound is amplified
it is made louder.

 sound

anaesthetic

Anaesthetics are chemicals that stop humans
or animals feeling pain.

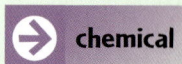 chemical

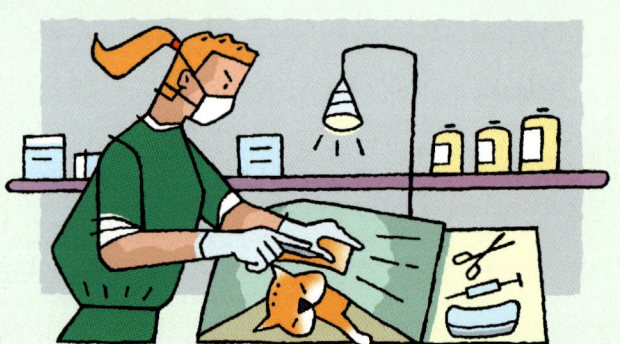

Vets and doctors use anaesthetics
on their patients.

animal

Animals are living things that have
senses. They can move some part of
themselves. Unlike plants they cannot
make their own food and have to eat
plants or other animals.

All of these are animals.

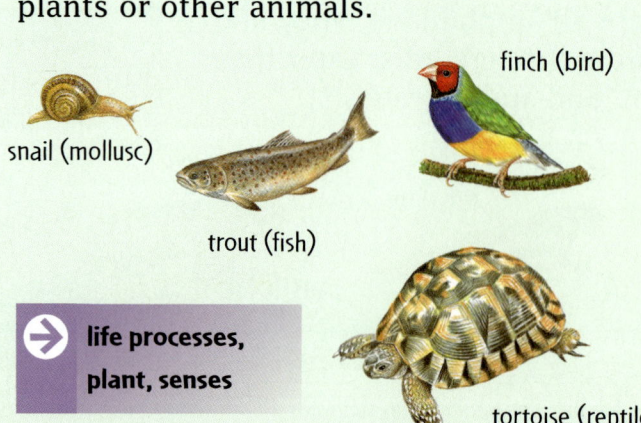

snail (mollusc)

trout (fish)

finch (bird)

life processes,
plant, senses

tortoise (reptile)

giraffe (mammal)

anther

Anthers are the pollen-producing male parts of a plant. They grow on the end of long filaments.

An anther and a filament taken together are called a stamen.

 flower, male, pollen, stamen

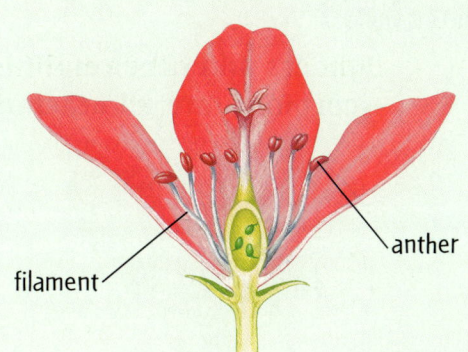

filament

anther

antibiotic

Antibiotics are medicines that kill bacteria. Antibiotics cannot kill viruses so are useless for treating colds.

 bacterium, cold, virus

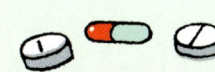

antiseptic

Antiseptics are substances that kill germs in cuts and wounds. If you do not kill germs they can cause cuts to go septic.

 **germ**

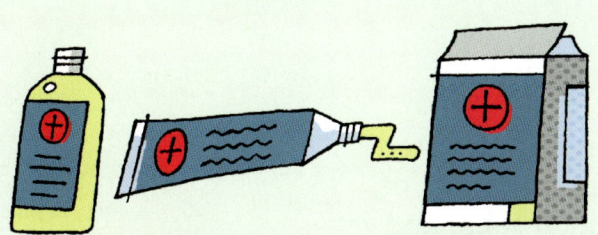

Antiseptics come as liquids, creams, and sprays.

anus

The anus is the hole at the end of the alimentary canal where waste food is pushed out.

 alimentary canal

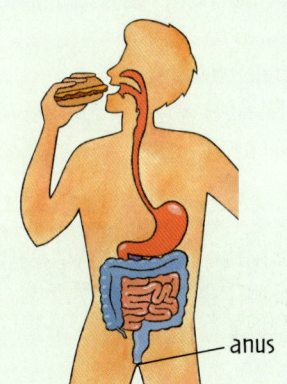

anus

arachnid

Spiders and other eight-legged animals, including scorpions, are all arachnids.

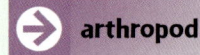

scorpion

spider
(tarantula)

All arachnids are arthropods.

artery

Arteries are blood vessels that carry blood away from the heart. Most arteries contain blood that is rich in oxygen.

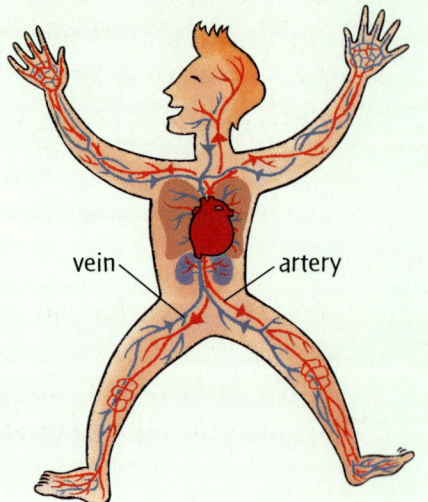

vein   artery

 capillary, heart, vein

arthropod

Arthropods are animals that have jointed legs and a hard outer skeleton instead of bones. Insects, spiders, crustaceans, and woodlice are all arthropods.

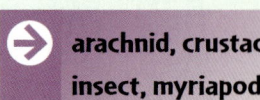 arachnid, crustacean, insect, myriapod

crab (crustacean)

beetle (insect)

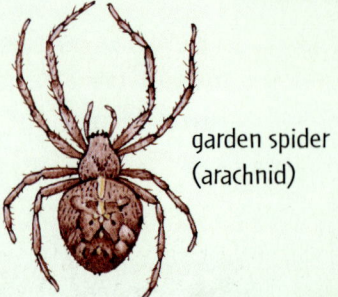

garden spider
(arachnid)

Arthropods do not have bony skeletons.

asteroid

Asteroids are rocky or metal objects that orbit the Sun. The biggest of them is about the size of Britain. Most are tiny.

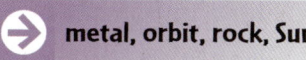
metal, orbit, rock, Sun

Most asteroids are found in the asteroid belt between Mars and Jupiter.

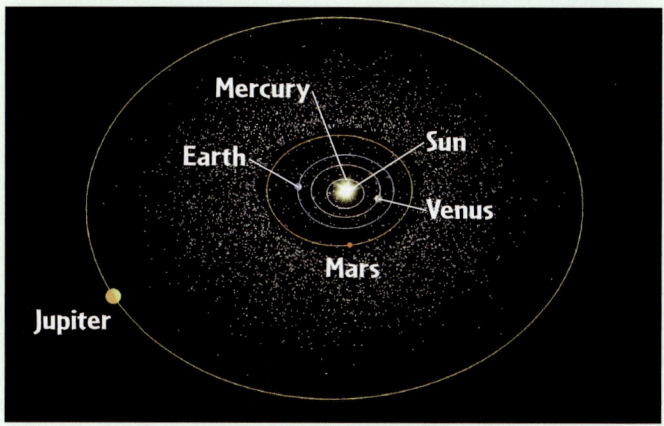

Mercury

Earth

Sun

Venus

Mars

Jupiter

asthma

Asthma is a disease where the airways in the lungs close up, making it difficult to breathe. Some people's asthma gets worse when they breathe in cigarette smoke.

lung

Medicines to help asthma are usually breathed in through an inhaler.

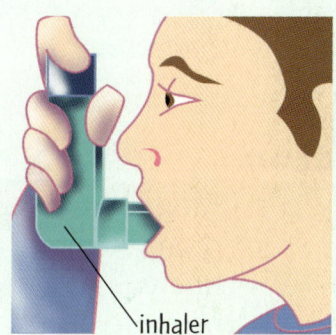
inhaler

astronomy

The study of the planets and stars is called astronomy.

planet, star, universe

atmosphere

The atmosphere is the air that surrounds planet Earth.

space

The atmosphere has several layers.

layers of atmosphere

Earth

air, Earth

atom

Atoms are the smallest particles of an element. Each atom has a nucleus in the middle, and one or more electrons going round it.

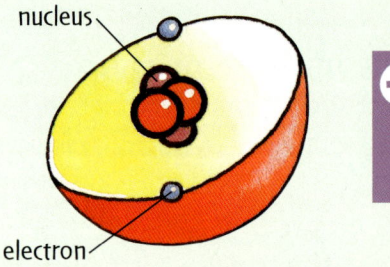

nucleus

electron

electron, element, nucleus

axis (plural axes)

The axis of the Earth is an imaginary line through the Earth from the North Pole to the South Pole. The Earth rotates around its axis.

Earth, seasons

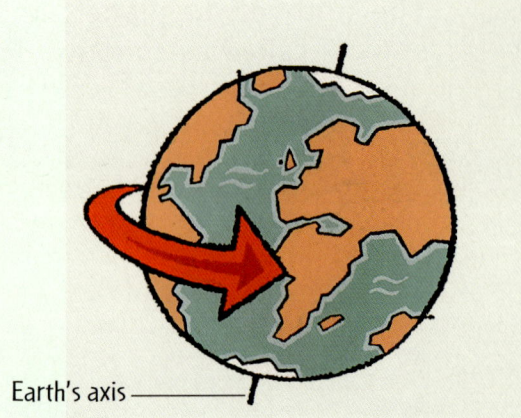

Earth's axis

Bb

bacterium (plural bacteria)

Bacteria are tiny living things. Some cause illness such as diarrhoea and earache. Others are used to help make compost, cheese, and yoghurt.

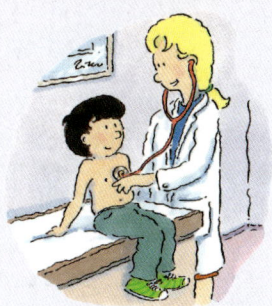

Bacteria can infect many parts of the body.

 antibiotic, germ, infect

balance

When two forces are equal they balance each other. The weight of a floating object is balanced by upthrust from the water.

This seesaw isn't balanced because one person is heavier than the other.

 centre of gravity, float, pivot

bark

Bark is the outer covering of a tree. The bark prevents disease from entering the wood of the tree.

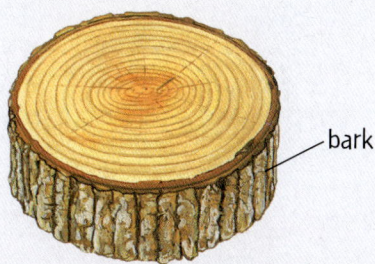

bark

barometer

Barometers are devices that show air pressure. High pressure usually means fine weather. Low pressure gives windy wet weather.

 **pressure**

battery

Batteries contain chemicals that produce an electrical current when connected in a circuit.

 chemical, circuit, current, electricity, volt

There are many different kinds of battery.

beak

The hard mouthparts of birds and some reptiles are called beaks. They are made of a material called chitin.

Birds have different types of beak, depending on what they eat.

 bird, reptile

curlew

pelican

finch

flamingo

eagle

beetle

Beetles are insects with hard wing cases covering their back.

 insect

ground beetle   tiger beetle   diving beetle

These are just three of the 300 000 different types of beetle.

bicarbonate of soda

Bicarbonate of soda is a chemical that fizzes when mixed with water. It is used in self-raising flour to produce light cakes.

 chemical

Big Bang

The Universe started with a huge explosion. Scientists call it the Big Bang.

 planets, star, Universe

Everything that makes up the planets and stars was created soon after the Big Bang.

binocular

Animals with binocular vision, such as people and owls, have two eyes looking forward.

 **animal, eye**

Animals with binocular vision can judge distances accurately.

biodegradable

Materials that break down and decay are biodegradable. Leaves and branches are biodegradable. Most plastic is not biodegradable but some is specially made to break down eventually.

 **decay**

biodiversity

Biodiversity is the variety of plants and animals in the world or in a habitat.

Plants and animals need biodiversity to survive.

biology

Biology is the study of plants, animals, and other living things.

→ **botany, life processes, zoology**

biped

Animals that walk on two legs are bipeds. All birds are bipedal.

→ **animal, bird**

Humans are the only mammals that are bipedal all the time.

bird

Birds are two-legged animals covered with feathers. All birds have wings but not all can fly. Ostriches and penguins, for instance, cannot fly.

→ **egg, feather**

emperor penguin

weaver bird and nest

blue tit

thrush

tern

duck

goose

swan

gull

All birds lay eggs, and many birds build nests.

black hole

Black holes are the remains of giant stars that have collapsed. Anything that comes close to a black hole is attracted in and is never seen again.

 mass, star

bladder

The bladder is an organ in the abdomen. Urine is stored there.

Urine travels to the bladder from the kidneys.

 abdomen, organ, urine

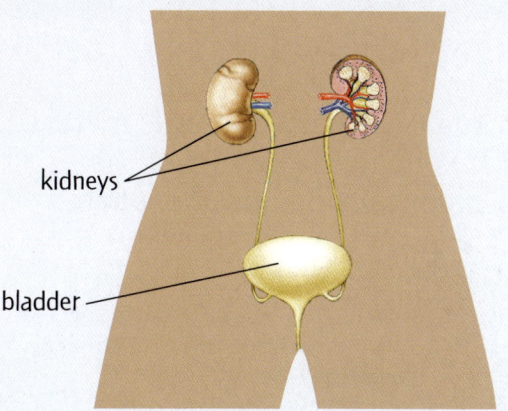

kidneys

bladder

blood

Blood is the red liquid that is pumped around our body by the heart. It carries oxygen, food, and water to all the parts of our body.

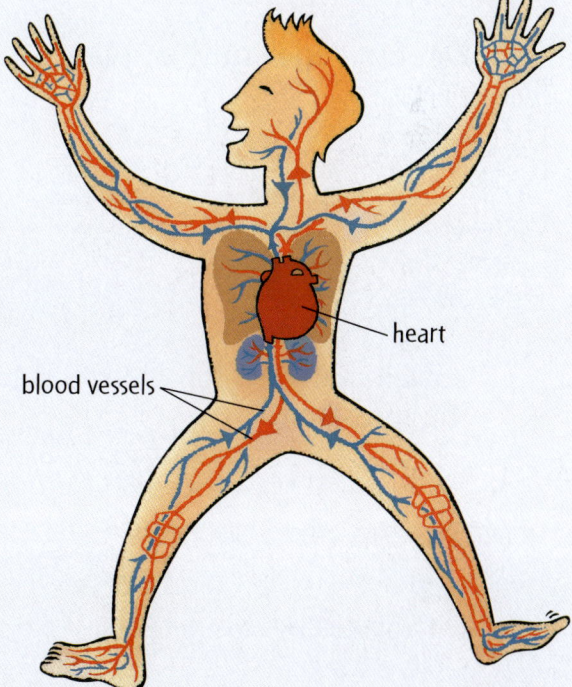

heart

blood vessels

artery, capillary, heart, oxygen, vein

boil

When a liquid reaches boiling point, bubbles of vapour are released. Water boils at 100°C.

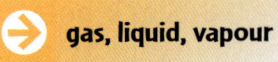
gas, liquid, vapour

When a liquid boils, bubbles are formed in all parts of the liquid.

bone

Bone is a hard and stiff material. It is made mainly from the chemical calcium phosphate.

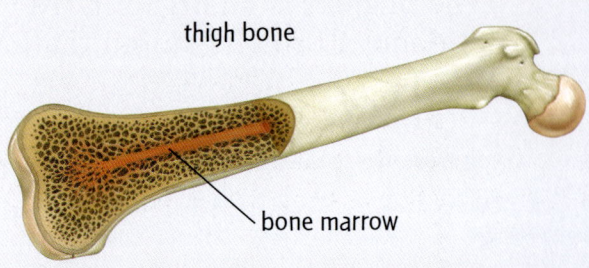
thigh bone

bone marrow

chemical

In the middle of some bones there is soft material called bone marrow.

botany

Botany is the study of plants.

flower
petal
stem
leaf
bud
root

biology, plant

bowel

Bowel is a word for the lower part of the intestines.

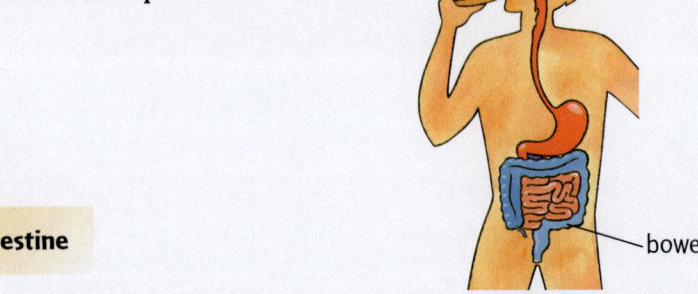
bowel

alimentary canal, intestine

brain

The brain is a mass of nerve tissue.
It is the organ we use to think.

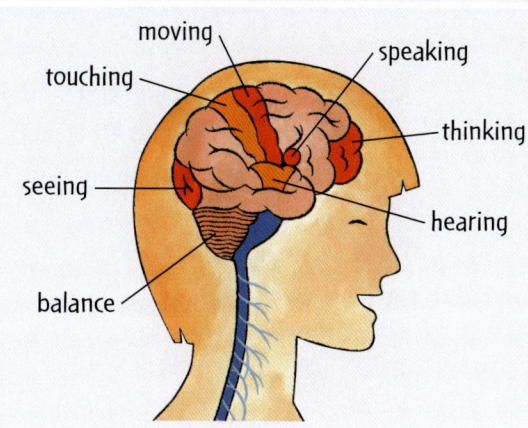

➡ **nerve, organ, tissue**

Different parts of the brain do different jobs.

breathe

Animals breathe by taking in air.
They use oxygen from the air to
help them get energy from food.
Animals get rid of another gas,
carbon dioxide, as they breathe out.

➡ **air**

blowing out a candle

breed

When a living thing breeds it produces young.

➡ **reproduction**

parents   breeding   young

brittle

Materials that are brittle do not bend easily. They snap or break into pieces.

Pottery is strong, but brittle.

 glass

bug

Bugs are insects with mouths that suck liquid.

 insect

The bed bug sucks blood and the aphid sucks plant sap.

bulb

A bulb is a short underground stem surrounded by thick, swollen leaves that store food for the plant.

Onion plants have bulbs. The onion leaves are folded inside the swollen bulb.

 plant

leaves

burn

When a chemical burns it produces a flame. The burning chemical combines with oxygen from the air. Another word for burning is combustion.

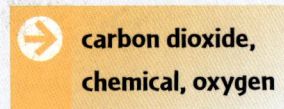 carbon dioxide, chemical, oxygen

The wax is burning and combining with oxygen to produce carbon dioxide.

Cc

cactus (plural cacti)

A cactus is a spiky plant that lives in very dry areas.

Cacti have thick stems to store water. Many have spikes instead of leaves.

caffeine

Caffeine is a drug found in coffee, some soft drinks, and tea.

 **drug**

Caffeine in coffee and tea might stop you sleeping well at night.

calcium

Calcium is one of the chemicals that forms our bones and teeth.

→ **bone, chemical, teeth**

jawbone

teeth

calorie

The calorie is the unit that measures the amount of energy in food. A 10-year-old needs about 2 400 calories of food energy each day.

Eating more calories than you use can make you overweight.

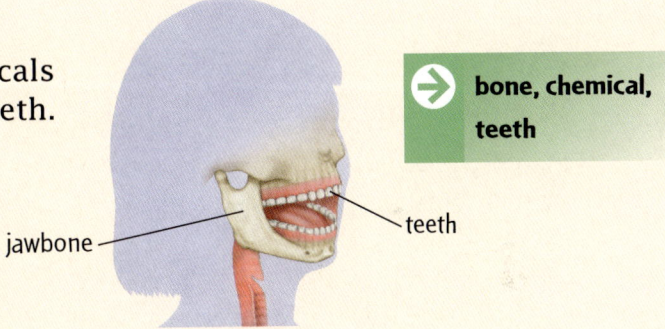

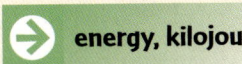 **energy, kilojoule**

calyx

The calyx is the green outer covering of a flower bud.

flower, sepal

The calyx is made up of sepals.

sepals

camera

Cameras let light onto a film to make photographs. Digital cameras record pictures using computer chips.

The lens focuses light on the film.

film

lens

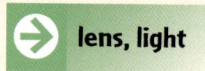

lens, light

camouflage

An animal that matches its background is camouflaged.

leaf insect

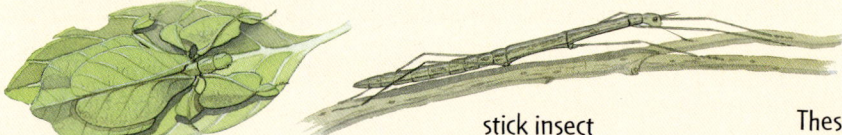

stick insect

These insects are camouflaged in leaves and twigs.

cancer

Cancer is an illness caused when cells in the body begin to grow in an unusual way.

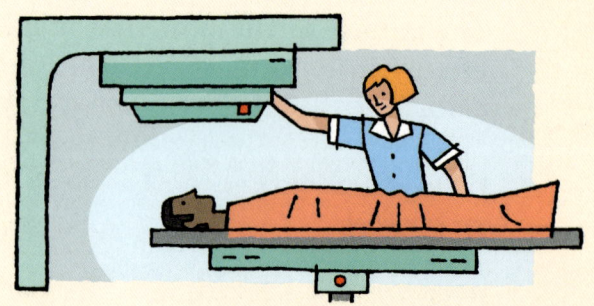

cell, radiation, reproduction

Cancers can be treated with medicines and radiation.

cannabis

Cannabis is a plant. It contains drugs. It is also called grass, hash, dagga, or dope.

→ drug

Cannabis contains drugs that affect the brain.

capillary

Capillaries are blood vessels. There are huge numbers of capillaries in our bodies. They are very thin and tiny amounts of blood flow through them.

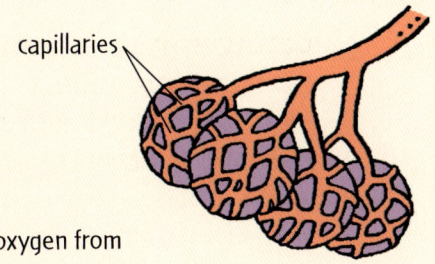

capillaries

→ artery, blood, vein

Capillaries in the lungs collect oxygen from the air and take it back to the heart.

carbohydrate

Carbohydrates are foods that give us energy.

These foods contain carbohydrates.

bread

maize

sugar

pasta

cereal

potato

→ energy

carbon

Carbon is an element. Our bodies are partly made up from carbon.

→ chemical, coal, diamond, element, graphite

Diamonds, soot, coal, and the graphite in pencil leads are all forms of carbon.

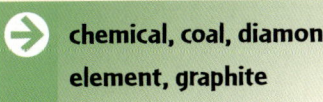

carbon dioxide

Carbon dioxide is a gas. It is a compound made from carbon and oxygen.

→ breathe, compound

Carbon dioxide can be used to put out fires.

carnivore

Carnivores are animals that eat other animals.

Many carnivores have sharp teeth and claws like this cheetah.

cheetah

caterpillar

Caterpillars are the larvae of butterflies and moths. A caterpillar hatches from an egg. When it has grown big enough, it becomes a chrysalis (pupa).

→ insect, larva, life cycle, metamorphosis, pupa

chrysalis

peacock butterfly

older caterpillar

young caterpillar

eggs

Caterpillars of the peacock butterfly eat nettle leaves.

cell

All living things are made up of cells. Most cells have a nucleus and a cell wall. Groups of cells form body tissue such as skin and muscle.

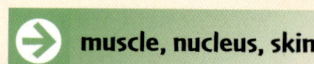

→ muscle, nucleus, skin

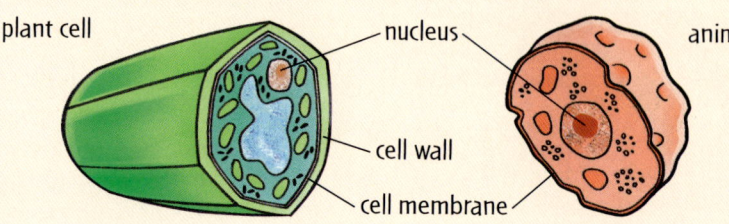

plant cell

nucleus

animal cell

cell wall

cell membrane

Plant cells have a tough cell wall, animal cells do not.

cell (electric)

An electric cell is the scientific name for a battery. A cell produces electrical current chemically.

 battery

Electric cells have different shapes for different uses.

Celsius

Temperature is measured in degrees Celsius (°C).

 boil, freeze, thermometer

The freezing point of water is 0 °C and its boiling point is 100 °C.

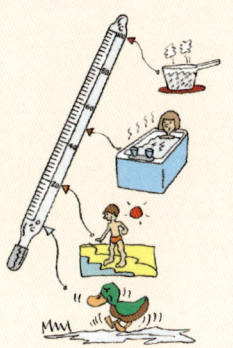

100°C boiling point

0°C freezing point

centre of gravity

The centre of gravity is the point around which an object balances.

 balance, gravity

high centre of gravity

low centre of gravity

Objects with a low centre of gravity are very stable. Objects with a high centre of gravity fall over easily.

ceramic

Ceramics are materials made of hardened clay or glass.

China cups, glasses, and flower pots are types of ceramic.

cereal

1. Cereals are plants such as oats, wheat, rice, maize, and barley.
2. We eat cereal seeds as bread, pasta, rice, and breakfast cereals.

 grass

Cereals are all
types of grass.

rice   oats   wheat   maize

chalk

Chalk is a white rock made from the
remains of tiny sea creatures. Chalk was
laid down millions of years ago, at the
time of the dinosaurs.

 dinosaur, rock

In some places chalk forms tall cliffs.

charcoal

Charcoal is the remains of partly burnt wood.
To make charcoal, wood is heated in a container
that has very little air in it.

 air, burn, wood

Charcoal leaves a black mark on paper.
Artists sometimes use it for drawing.

chemical

Chemicals are substances made in laboratories and
factories. They include medicines and plastics.
The cells of living things are full of other kinds of
chemicals. They are like tiny chemical factories.

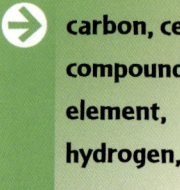 **carbon, cell, compound, element, hydrogen, oxygen**

Some foods have chemicals added
to keep them fresh.

chemistry

Chemistry is the study of materials and the way they change when they react together.

Chemists can purify a liquid by distilling it.

➡ **chemical, distil, react**

chlorophyll

The green of plant leaves is due to a chemical called chlorophyll. Plants need chlorophyll to photosynthesize.

Green leaves contain chlorophyll. In the autumn, the leaves of many trees lose their chlorophyll.

➡ **photosynthesis**

chromosome

Chromosomes are strands of material in cells that tell the body how to develop. They are made of genes.

➡ **cell, gene, nucleus**

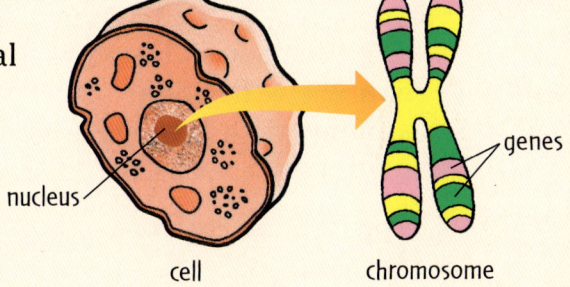

genes

nucleus

cell

chromosome

chrysalis

Chrysalis is another word for pupa.

The chrysalis is the resting stage as a caterpillar changes to an adult.

➡ **caterpillar, larva, life cycle, metamorphosis, pupa**

caterpillar

chrysalis (pupa)

cigarette

A cigarette is a tube of paper filled with tobacco.

Many smokers are addicted to the nicotine in tobacco.

→ **addict, nicotine**

circuit

A circuit is a complete path that an electric current can flow around. Electricity flows from the battery, through wires and devices before returning to the battery.

→ **battery**

Circuit a) is complete and electricity can flow. Circuit b) is not complete so the bulb is not lit.

classify

Living things are classified into groups. For instance:
- animals with bones are classified as vertebrates
- animals with six legs are classified as insects
- plants with seeds on cones are classified as conifers.

→ **conifer, insect, vertebrate**

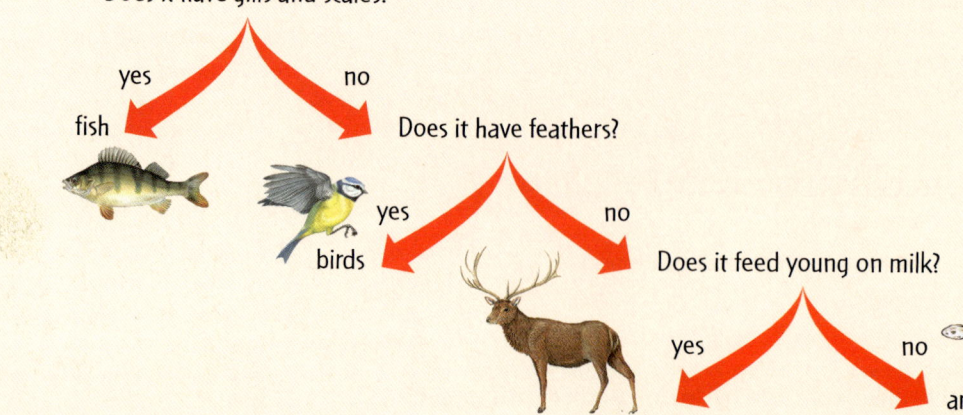

Does it have gills and scales?

yes   no

fish   Does it have feathers?

yes   no

birds   Does it feed young on milk?

yes   no

mammals   amphibian or reptile

clay

Clay is a type of earth that is sticky when wet. It can be formed into different shapes.

Clay is used to make pottery and ceramic things such as cups.

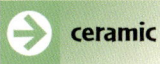 ceramic

climate

The climate of a place is the most usual weather it has over many years.

 weather

This desert has a hot, dry climate, but occasionally it has rainy weather.

cloud

Clouds are made up of billions of tiny water drops. These drops fall as rain when they get heavy enough.

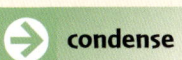 condense

Dark storm clouds bring rain.

coal

Coal is a shiny black rock made from the remains of trees that lived millions of years ago.

Coal began to form in swampy forests about 300 million years ago.

 carbon, dinosaur, mineral, rock

cocoon

Cocoons are a type of chrysalis or pupa. They are made from threads that are spun by the caterpillar.

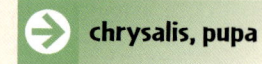
→ **chrysalis, pupa**

Silk comes from the cocoons of silk moth caterpillars. Each has many metres of thread which is used to make silk clothes.

cold

1. A person with a cold has a runny nose and feels unwell. Colds are caused by a virus.

2. Cold is the absence of heat.

→ **heat, virus**

cold-blooded

Cold-blooded animals cannot keep their bodies warm without heat from the Sun or from their surroundings.

chameleon

sailfish

Reptiles and fish are cold-blooded.

colour

White light can be split into the colours of the rainbow. In a TV red, green, and blue coloured light is mixed together to make white and all the other colours of the spectrum.

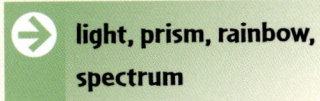
light, prism, rainbow, spectrum

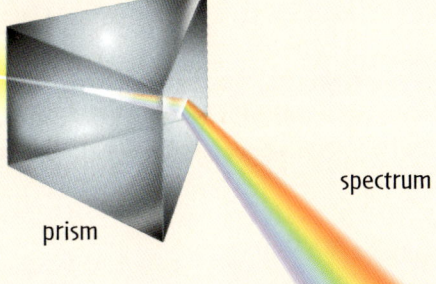

white light

prism

spectrum

A prism can split white light into a spectrum of colours.

comet

A comet is a ball of ice orbiting the Sun. From Earth, comets look like bright stars. We can only see the tails on very bright comets.

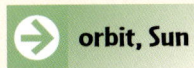
orbit, Sun

Bright comets can be seen from the Earth about every ten years.

compass (magnetic)

A compass needle always points north and south. The needle is a magnet. It is attracted by the magnetic poles of the Earth.

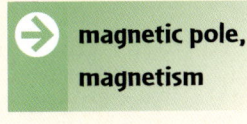
magnetic pole, magnetism

compost

Compost is a mixture in which you grow plants. Compost can be made using soil, peat, or coconut fibre. Compost can also be made by rotting down garden clippings, and manure from animals.

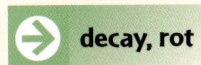
decay, rot

The weed can go on the compost heap as it will rot. The plastic will not make compost.

compound

A combination of two elements is called a compound. Water is a compound made from oxygen and hydrogen. Carbon dioxide is a compound of carbon and oxygen.

→ **atom, carbon, element, hydrogen, oxygen**

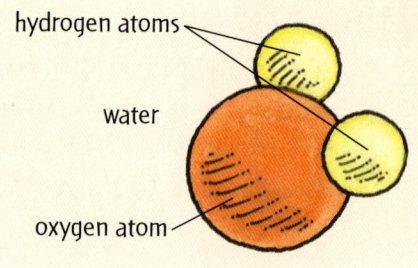

hydrogen atoms

water

oxygen atom

This drawing shows the way that water is a compound of hydrogen and oxygen atoms.

compress

To compress something is to press or squeeze it by a force so that it takes up less space.

concave

Concave means curved inwards, like the inside of a ball or circle. Mirrors or lenses that dip inwards are called concave. The opposite of concave is convex.

→ **convex, lens, mirror, reflect**

A concave lens spreads light.

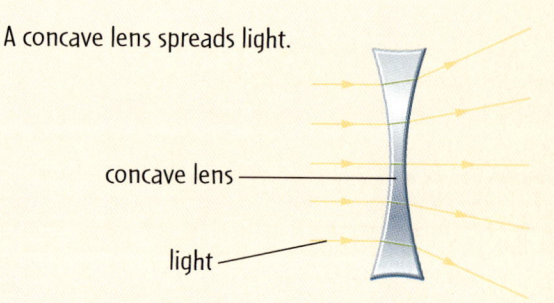

concave lens

light

concentrate

A concentrated solution is stronger than a dilute one.

→ **dilute, solution**

concentrated juice

dilute juice

The opposite of concentrate is dilute.

condense

When water vapour condenses on a surface it changes from a gas to a liquid. Condensation often happens when damp air meets a cold surface.

 gas, liquid, state of matter

Running a bath causes condensation on the mirror.

condom

A condom is a rubber tube that is placed over the penis. It is closed at one end to catch sperm. This stops them reaching an egg to fertilize it.

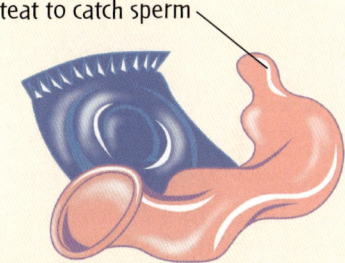

teat to catch sperm

 egg, fertilize, penis, sperm

conduct (electricity)

Materials that conduct electricity allow it to pass through.

All metals conduct electricity. Carbon and silicon conduct too, but not as well as metals.

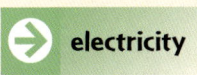 **electricity**

conduct (heat)

Materials that let heat pass through easily are good conductors of heat.

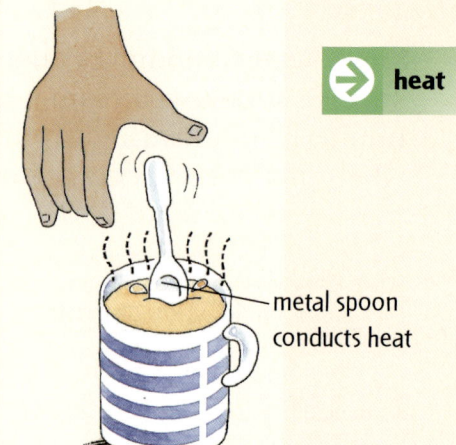

heat

All metals are good conductors of heat.
Wood and plastic are poor conductors.

metal spoon conducts heat

conifer

A conifer is a plant that carries its seeds on cones. Most conifers are evergreen.

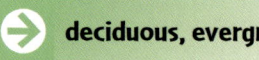
deciduous, evergreen, seed

cone

The Scots pine is a conifer tree.

conservation

Trying to stop animals and plants from dying out is known as conservation. Conservationists are people who try to stop living things becoming extinct.

mountain gorilla

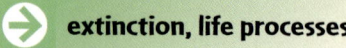
extinction, life processes

All these animals will die out without conservation.

tiger

panda

constipation

If people have a problem in passing faeces they have constipation.

A diet of high-fibre foods like these should help avoid constipation.

 faeces, fibre

contract

When something contracts, it becomes smaller. The opposite of contract is expand.

Metals like mercury contract when they get cooler.

 **expand**

convection

When gases or liquids are heated they become lighter. This makes them rise and move. This movement is called convection.

The warm air rises and moves round the room. It sinks as it cools.

 conduct (heat), radiation

convex

Convex means curved outwards, like the outside of a ball or circle. Mirrors or lenses that bulge out are convex. Convex mirrors give a wide angle of view.

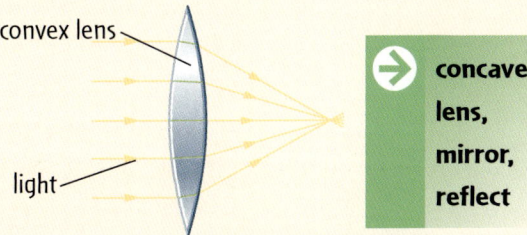

convex lens

light

concave, lens, mirror, reflect

A convex lens concentrates light. The opposite of convex is concave.

copper

Copper is a reddish-brown metal. It is easy to bend and is a very good conductor of heat and electricity.

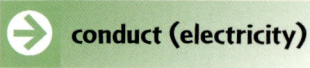

conduct (electricity)

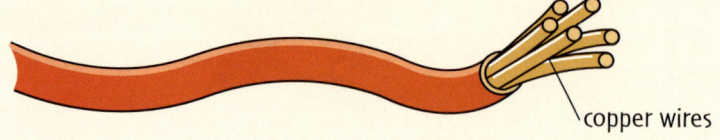

copper wires

Electric wires are made of copper.

coral

Coral are tiny animals that live in tropical seas. They live in groups fixed to the sea bottom.

animal

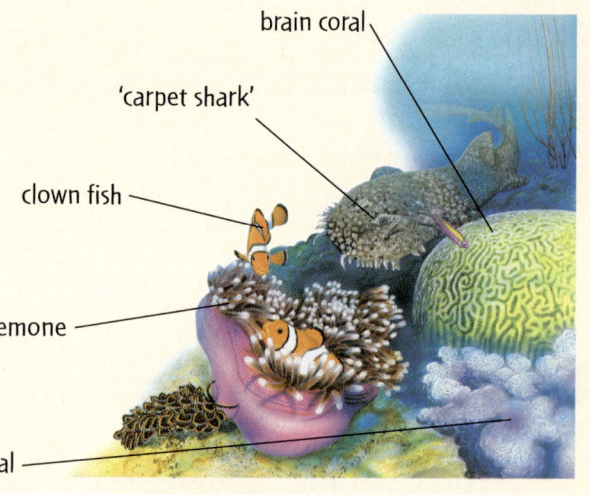

brain coral

'carpet shark'

clown fish

sea anemone

Many sea creatures
live on coral reefs.

branching coral

cork

The bark of some oak trees is made of a thick layer of cork.

Large pieces of bark can be taken from cork trees without killing the tree.

bark

corrosion

Corrosion happens when chemicals cause a metal to be worn away.

metal, rust

Iron or steel rusting is one kind of corrosion.

cranium

The top part of the skull is called the cranium.

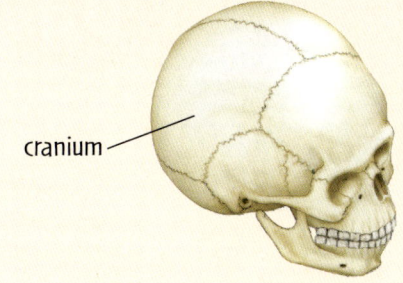

cranium

The brain is protected by the cranium.

→ **bone, brain, skull**

crustacean

Crustaceans are animals that usually have a hard shell and many legs. They are a type of arthropod.

→ **arthropod, invertebrate**

crab

shrimp

Crabs and shrimps are common crustaceans. Most crustaceans live in the sea.

crystal

A crystal is a mineral with a regular shape and a glassy appearance.

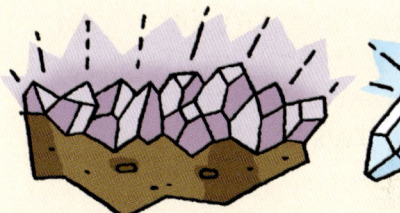

→ **diamond, mineral**

The faces of a crystal are flat and reflect the light beautifully.

current (electricity)

A flow of electricity is called a current. The units used to measure current are called amps.

→ **amp, battery, electricity**

The current is the same at each point in a circuit.

Dd

data

Data is information.

Data is stored in many different ways.

day

A day lasts for 24 hours. This is the time it takes for the Earth to rotate once on its axis.

➡ **axis, night, rotate**

dead

A living thing is dead if it cannot do the things that living things are able to do. Living things can move, reproduce, use their senses, grow, breathe, and feed.

A big tree may stay standing long after it has died.

➡ **alive, breathe, excrete, life processes, reproduction**

decay

When a living thing dies bacteria and fungi make it decay. The chemicals released by decay are used by new living things.

➡ **bacterium, biodegradable, chemical, decompose, fungus, life processes**

deciduous

Trees that lose their leaves once each year are deciduous.

 evergreen, leaf

decompose

A dead plant or animal decomposes as it rots away.

Beetles, worms, and other minibeasts help this carpet of autumn leaves to decompose.

 bacterium, compost, decay, fungus, rot

density

Materials with a high density are heavy for their size. Materials with a low density are light for their size.

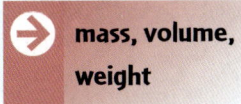 mass, volume, weight

low density   high density

Lead has a high density. It weighs much more than the same volume of polystyrene.

dew

Dew drops form when water condenses out of the air. Dew covers plants on cool mornings.

 condense, state of matter, water

diabetes

Diabetes is a disease that stops people digesting sugar properly.

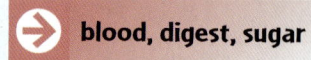 blood, digest, sugar

Diabetics don't have enough of a substance called insulin in their bodies. Many have to have regular injections of insulin.

diamond

Diamond is a beautiful, hard, clear type of crystal. It is made from carbon.

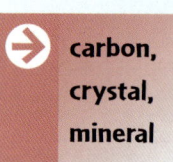 carbon, crystal, mineral

Diamonds are used in expensive jewellery.

diarrhoea

Diarrhoea is runny and loose faeces. It is often caused by bacteria in the intestines.

 bacterium, faeces, intestine

diet

Diet is the sort of food animals or people regularly eat.

 food

A food pyramid is a guide to a healthy diet.

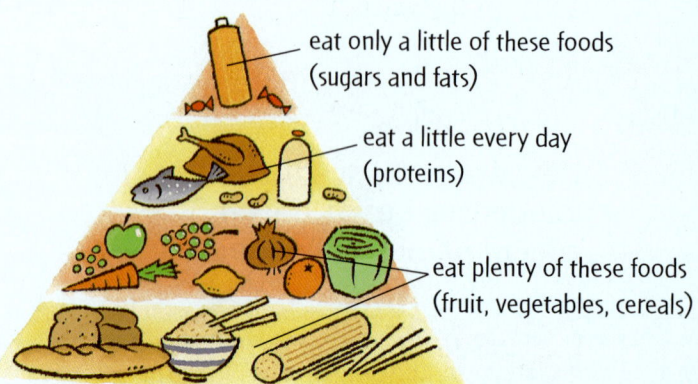

eat only a little of these foods (sugars and fats)

eat a little every day (proteins)

eat plenty of these foods (fruit, vegetables, cereals)

digest

The stomach and intestines digest food. This means that they soften and change food so that the body can absorb it.

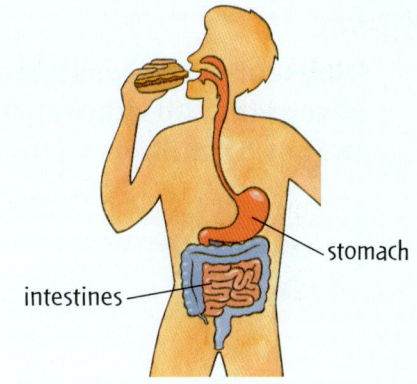

stomach

intestines

food, intestine, stomach

digital

Devices that use numbers to show or store information are digital. CDs store music in digital form.

This computer stores information digitally.

Digital watches do not have a dial.

dilute

When a solution is diluted it is made weaker.

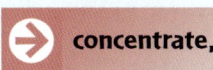
concentrate, solution

concentrated juice

diluted juice

The opposite of dilute is concentrate.

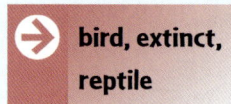

dinosaur

Dinosaurs are an extinct group of reptiles. All dinosaurs became extinct 65 million years ago.

→ **bird, extinct, reptile**

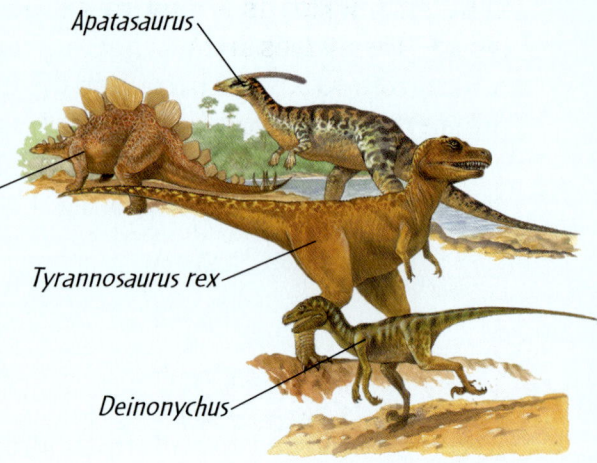

Apatasaurus

Stegosaurus

Tyrannosaurus rex

Deinonychus

Birds are related to the dinosaurs.

disease

When a person is ill or sick, they may have a disease.

→ **AIDS, cold, diabetes, joint**

Arthritis is a disease that affects the joints.

dissolve

A solid that completely mixes in with a liquid and cannot be seen has dissolved. This mixture of solid and liquid is a solution.

→ **liquid, saturated, solid, solute, solution**

Water with salt in it is clear like pure water, but you can taste the salt.

distil

Distilling water is a way to get rid of impurities in it.
- The liquid is heated.
- The vapour produced is then condensed (distilled).
- The condensed liquid is pure.

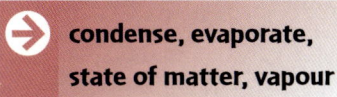 condense, evaporate, state of matter, vapour

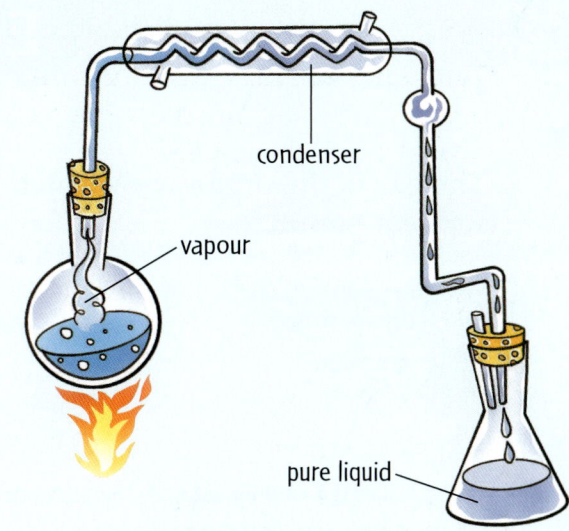

condenser

vapour

pure liquid

DNA

DNA is a substance that contains all the information for our cells to reproduce correctly.

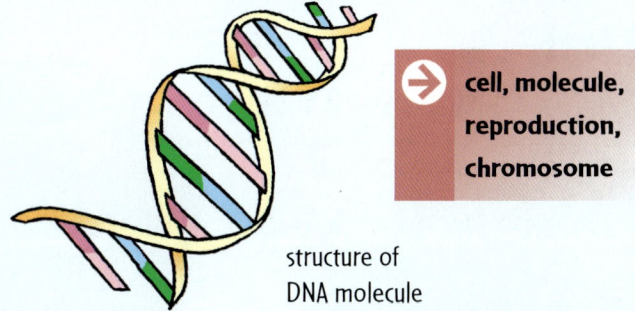

cell, molecule, reproduction, chromosome

structure of DNA molecule

DNA is found in chromosomes inside our cells. DNA stands for deoxyribonucleic acid.

drug

A drug is a substance that has an effect in a person's body.

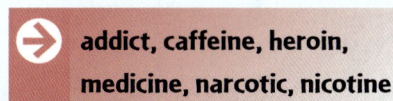 addict, caffeine, heroin, medicine, narcotic, nicotine

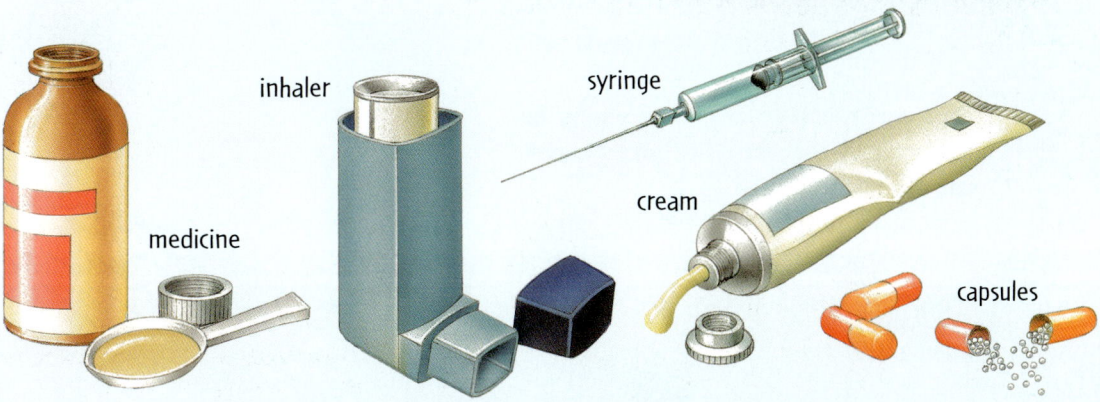

inhaler

syringe

cream

medicine

capsules

Many drugs are also medicines. They can be taken in many ways.

47

Ee

ear

The ear is the organ with which we hear sound.

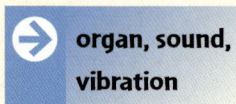 organ, sound, vibration

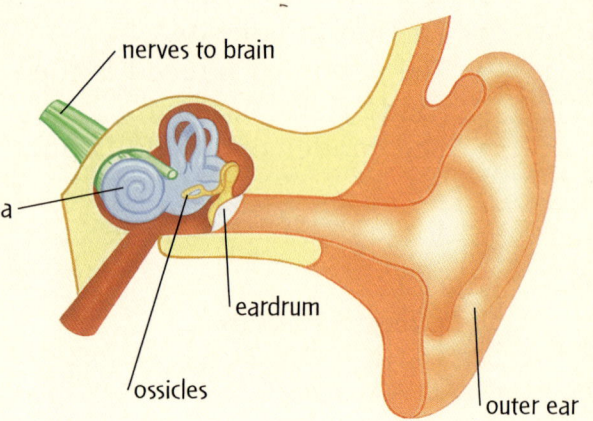

nerves to brain

cochlea

eardrum

ossicles

outer ear

Sound makes the eardrum vibrate. This vibration is passed on to the cochlea and the brain.

Earth

The planet on which we live is the Earth.

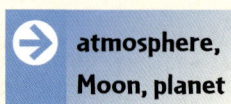 atmosphere, Moon, planet

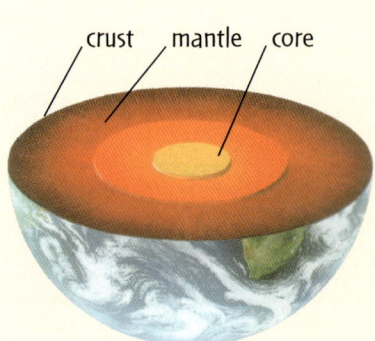

crust mantle core

echo

An echo is heard when sound bounces back off a wall or cliff.

There is a delay between the sound leaving the source and us hearing the echo. This is because sound takes time to travel.

 sound

eclipse

An eclipse happens when the Moon is directly in front of the Sun. It blocks the sunlight from reaching the Earth.

 lunar, Moon, Sun

When the Moon covers the Sun, you see the glow caused by the Sun's burning atmosphere (the corona) around the edge of the Moon.

ecology

Ecology is the study of living things and the way they live in their environment.

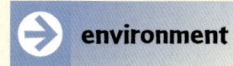 **environment**

These students are studying the sorts of plants that live in different places.

ecosystem

An ecosystem includes the living things and non-living things in one place, and their relationship to each other.

soil   pebbles   air   frog   fish   weeds

eczema

Eczema is a skin disease that causes the skin to be very dry and sore.

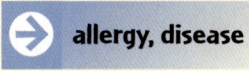 **allergy, disease**

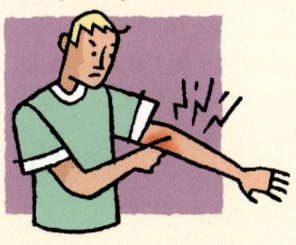

This disease can be caused by an allergy to pets or to certain foods.

egg

An egg is a roundish object that female animals produce. An egg can develop into a new baby animal if it is fertilized. In mammals eggs grow inside the mother.

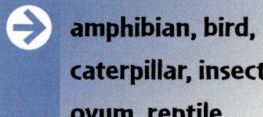
amphibian, bird, caterpillar, insect, ovum, reptile

barn owl chick

Birds' eggs have a hard shell. Reptiles' eggs are leathery.

elastic

Materials that are elastic spring back into their original shape.

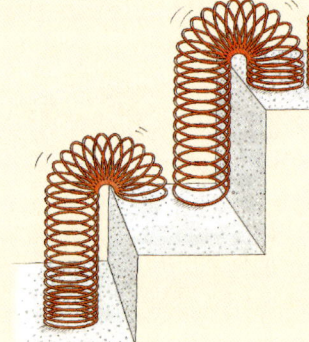

This spring is elastic.

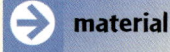
material

electricity

Electricity is a form of energy used for lighting, heating, making sound, and making machines work.

battery, conduct (electricity), current, energy, work

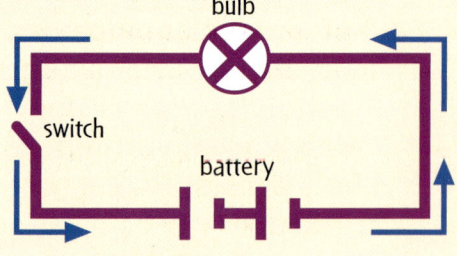

bulb

switch

battery

Some of the energy works in the bulb to make it hot.

electric symbols

Each electric device has a symbol to save you drawing a picture each time.

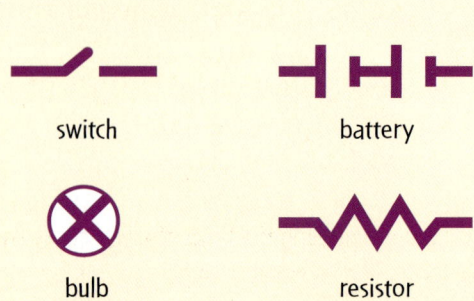

switch

battery

bulb

resistor

electron

Electrons are parts of atoms.

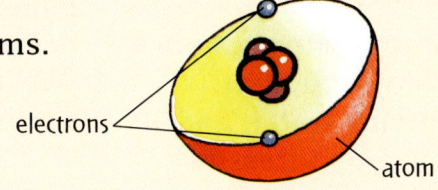

electrons

atom

atom

element

Elements are the basic parts of all materials.
There are over 100 different elements.
Elements combine to make compounds.

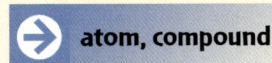
atom, compound

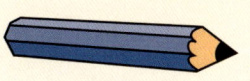

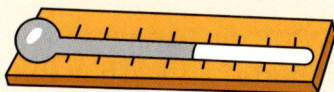

Pencil leads are made
from the element carbon.

Mercury is a liquid element
used in thermometers.

Oxygen gas is the element
we need to breathe.

embryo

1. An embryo is the offspring
of an animal before it is born
or comes out of an egg.

2. An embryo is a plant that is
beginning to grow from a seed.

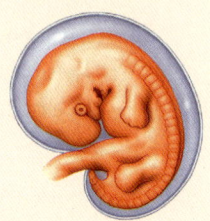

This embryo is
about 6 weeks old.

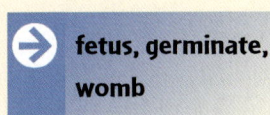
fetus, germinate,
womb

energy

Energy is the ability to do work.

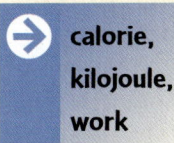
calorie,
kilojoule,
work

Energy can be in the form of electrical energy,
food energy, heat, or movement energy.

energy (renewable)

Renewable energy supplies are those that will not run out. The wind, running water, and the Sun can all be sources of renewable energy.

hydroelectric (water) energy

wind energy

solar energy

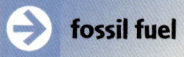
→ fossil fuel

environment

The environment is the conditions in which a living thing exists. Soil, climate, and other living things all count as part of the environment.

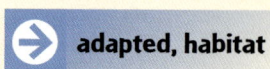
→ adapted, habitat

Rainforest plants need a wet environment. These plants live on a tree branch.

equinox

The equinox happens on the days that are halfway between midwinter and midsummer. On the equinox, every place on Earth has 12 hours of daylight and 12 hours of night.

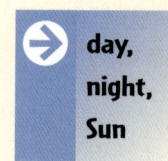
→ day, night, Sun

MARCH 21   SEPTEMBER 23

Equinoxes happen in autumn and spring.

erosion

Water and wind wear away at rocks and soil. This process is called erosion.

 rock

Water and wind have eroded the rocks in Monument Valley, USA, into these shapes.

evaporate

When water evaporates it changes from a liquid to vapour.

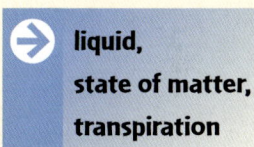 liquid, state of matter, transipration

Water evaporates more quickly when it is warm and windy.

evergreen

Trees and bushes that do not lose their leaves in winter are evergreen. Holly, pine trees, and ivy are evergreen plants.

In tropical countries where there is little difference between the seasons many of the plants are evergreen.

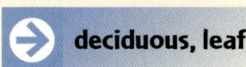 deciduous, leaf

evolution

Evolution is the way in which plants and animals have changed over millions of years.

50 million years ago

35 million years ago

How elephants evolved.

 bird, dinosaur, extinct, reptile

20 million years ago

African elephant today

excrete

Animals use their kidneys to filter waste from the blood. They excrete this in the form of urine.

 urine

exercise

People and other animals must exercise by moving if they are to stay healthy.

 aerobic

There are many different ways to exercise.

expand

When something expands, it becomes larger. The opposite of expand is contract.

Heat makes the mercury in a thermometer expand.

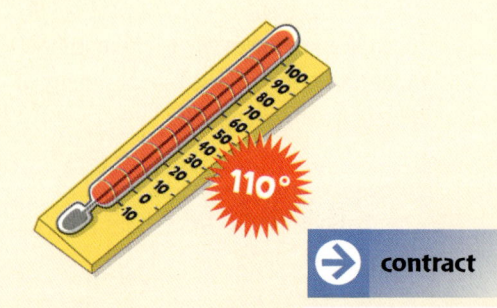

 contract

experiment

In an experiment you try something to see what happens.

In this experiment the student will find out how long the candle will burn in different-sized jars.

explosion

An explosion is when a substance burns very rapidly. It gives a sudden burst of energy.

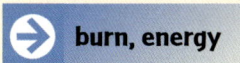
→ burn, energy

Fireworks are full of gunpowder, which explodes when they are set alight.

extinct

Animals and plants that have died out completely are extinct.

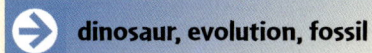
→ dinosaur, evolution, fossil

These animals have all become extinct in the last few hundred years.

passenger pigeon

moa

quagga

Tasmanian wolf

dodo

eye

The eye detects light. Light enters through the pupil. It passes through a lens which focuses light on the retina. Messages pass down the optic nerve.

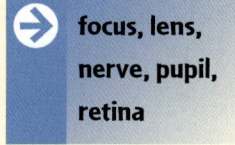
→ focus, lens, nerve, pupil, retina

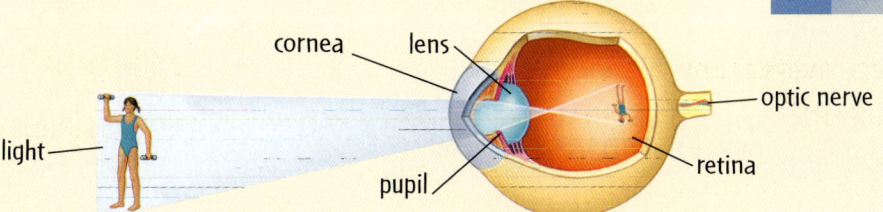

cornea · lens · optic nerve · light · pupil · retina

Ff

faeces

Animals make solid waste in the form of faeces.

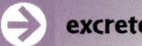
excrete

Cats will usually bury their faeces.

fat

People and many other animals have a layer of fat under their skin. This is a reserve for when food is scarce. Fat is found in foods like margarine and cheese and in some plant seeds.

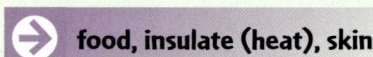
food, insulate (heat), skin

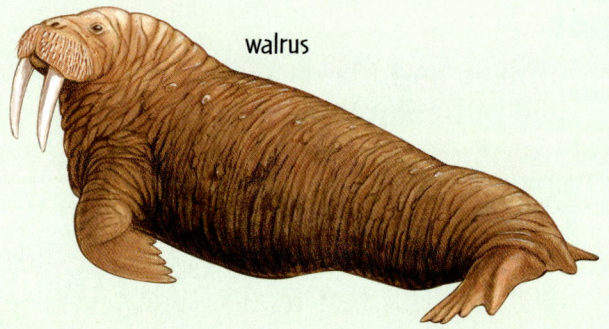
walrus

Fat insulates an animal. Animals that live in very cold water need thick layers of fat to keep them warm.

feather

Only birds have feathers. Feathers keep birds warm by insulating their skin.

shaft

barbs

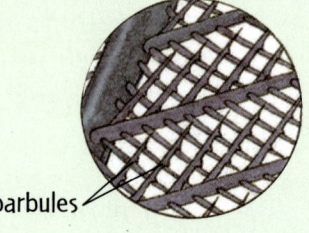
barbules

bird, insulate (heat), warm-blooded

The barbules zip together to form a light sheet of feather.

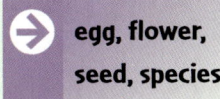

female

The female of a species is the sex that makes eggs or seeds. Usually female animals look after the young.

→ egg, flower, seed, species

ferment

When sugar or carbohydrates ferment they are changed into alcohol and carbon dioxide. Yeast is a fungus that is used to ferment sugar in bread, beer, and wine.

→ alcohol, carbohydrate, carbon dioxide, sugar

Yeast ferments the flour and produces bubbles of carbon dioxide. These bubbles are trapped in the dough and make the bread light.

fertilize

When the male sperm reaches the female egg it fertilizes it. The same thing happens in plants when the male pollen reaches the female ovule.

Only one male sperm will actually fertilize the female egg. Only a fertilized egg can develop into young.

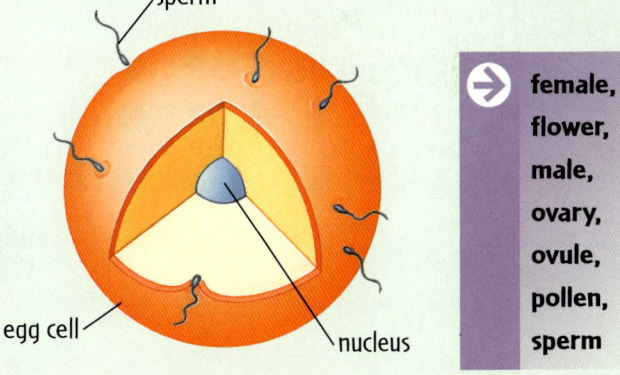

sperm

egg cell

nucleus

→ female, flower, male, ovary, ovule, pollen, sperm

fetus

An unborn baby that has been in the womb for more than eight weeks is called a fetus. Before that time it is known as an embryo.

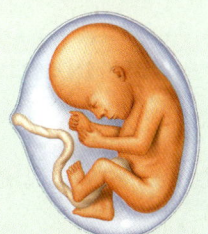

→ embryo, womb

This fetus is about 3 months old.

fibre

Fibre is part of a healthy diet. It passes through the intestines unchanged. It can stop people being constipated.

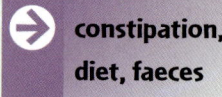
constipation, diet, faeces

Fruit, vegetables, and wholemeal flour have lots of fibre.

filter

Filters separate solids mixed in a liquid. Filters cannot separate solids that are in solution.

filter

The solid materials are caught in the filter but the coffee solution passes through.

 solution

fire

To get a fire going you need fuel, air, and heat. To put it out you must cool it, starve it of air, or remove the fuel.

air, flame, fuel

fish

Fish have backbones like all vertebrates.

A fish is an animal with a backbone. It has scales covering its body. It lives in water and breathes through gills.

fins

 gill, scale, vertebrate

gills

tail

flame

A flame is produced when something burns.

Solids and liquids do not burn directly. They have to produce a gas, and it is this that burns.

 burn, fire, gas

float

When an object floats it is being supported by water or air. The force that makes objects float is called upthrust.

 hot air balloon, submarine, upthrust

full tanker   empty tanker

A full tanker floats lower in the water than an empty one.

flower

A flower is a plant's way to reproduce. Once it has been fertilized, the flower produces fruit and seeds.

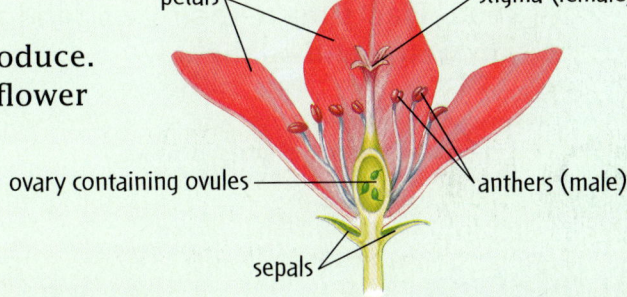

petals — stigma (female)

ovary containing ovules

anthers (male)

sepals

 anther, female, fertilize, male, ovule, pollen, seed

The male anthers produce pollen. The pollen fertilizes the female ovule.

fluid

A fluid is a gas or liquid that moves freely.

Milk and oil are fluids.

 carbon dioxide, gas, liquid

focus

When light is focused it makes a clear image. The lens in a camera focuses the image on the film.

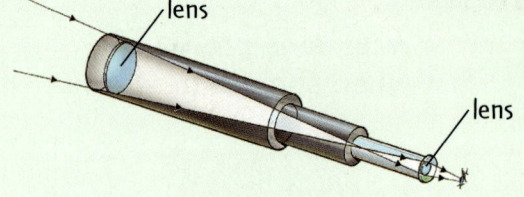

→ **image, lens, light**

The lenses in a telescope focus light from distant objects onto the eye.

fog

Clouds and fog are made from tiny droplets of liquid water.

→ **condense**

food

Food gives living things energy. Animals need to eat plants or other animals for food. Plants make their own food from air, water, and sunlight.

→ **diet, energy, photosynthesis**

food chain

Animals eat plants or other animals. The way this happens is shown in a food chain.

kestrel

mouse

grass

→ **animal, food, food web, plant**

Mice eat grass and seeds. Kestrels eat mice.

food pyramid

See diet.

food web

A food web shows the way that food chains are linked.

→ **animal, food, food chain, plant**

In the cold Antarctic seas, animals and plants depend on each other for food.

killer whale

right whale

sperm whale

leopard seal

albatross

walrus

crabeater seal

penguin

squid

fish

tiny plants

tiny animals

krill

force

A force is a push or a pull. Forces make objects start to move, slow down, or change direction.

→ **accelerate, air resistance, friction, gravity, magnetism**

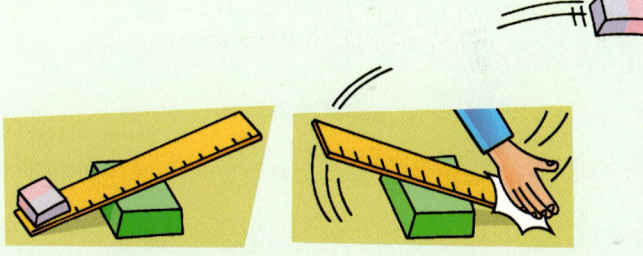

The force of your hand hitting one end of the ruler sends the rubber flying off the other end.

fossil

The bones or other remains of living things are sometimes preserved in rocks as fossils.

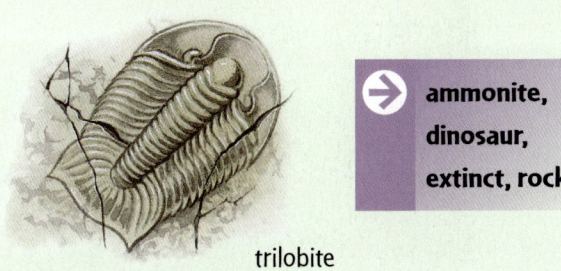

→ **ammonite, dinosaur, extinct, rock**

Fossils can be millions of years old. They tell us about life in the past.

trilobite

fossil fuel

Coal, oil, and gas are all fossil fuels. They were formed millions of years ago. Once they are used up they are not renewed.

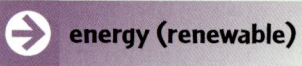
energy (renewable)

At the moment we depend for most of our energy on burning fossil fuel.

coal-fired power station

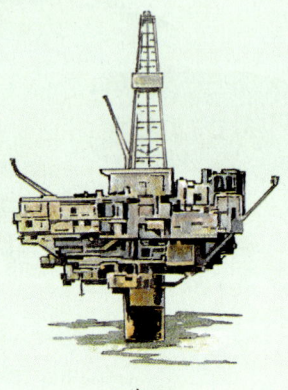

oil rig

freeze

When a liquid becomes cold enough to turn solid, it freezes. Chocolate freezes at room temperature, while water freezes at 0˚C.

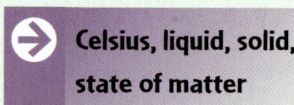
Celsius, liquid, solid, state of matter

Orange juice can be frozen to make lollies.

freshwater

Freshwater does not contain salt.

salt, water

Most lake and river water is freshwater but 99% of the water on Earth is salty.

friction

When one surface moves against another the rubbing force that tries to stop them is called friction. Friction slows all moving objects and gives off heat.

→ **force**

Friction helps tyres grip the road.

Friction stops you when you put the brakes on.

frost

Frost is frozen condensation. It happens when the air temperature is below 0 °C. Ground frost happens when the ground is colder than the air.

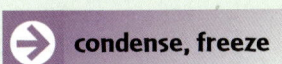
→ **condense, freeze**

When it is really cold, frost can turn the trees white.

fruit

The fruit of a plant is formed from its ovary. It protects the seeds. Animals are attracted to eat the fruit and spread the seed.

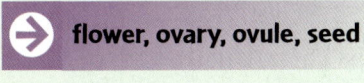
→ **flower, ovary, ovule, seed**

orange

pea

strawberry

maple tree

Some different types of fruit.

fuel

Fuel is a substance that can be burned to give heat or light. Most fuels contain carbon compounds.

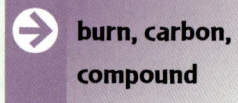

→ **burn, carbon, compound**

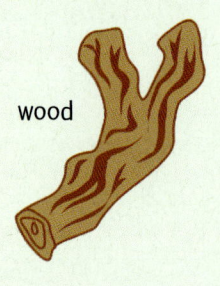

wood

petrol

Fuels may be solid, liquid, or gas.

fungus (plural fungi)

Fungi are a group of living things that are neither plants nor animals. A fungus looks like a plant, but it does not contain chlorophyll. Some fungi are poisonous.

shaggy ink cap

mushroom

bracket fungus

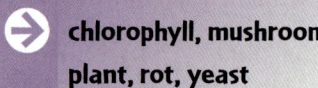

→ **chlorophyll, mushroom, plant, rot, yeast**

Fungi cannot make their own food and so have to live on other dead or living organisms.

fuse

A fuse is an electrical device that contains a thin piece of wire. The wire melts if the electric current going through it gets too big.

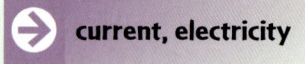

→ **current, electricity**

Fuses are a safety feature of all plugs and most electrical appliances.

3A

fuse

Gg

galaxy

A galaxy is an enormous group of stars. There may be billions of stars in a single galaxy.

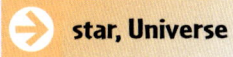 star, Universe

Our Solar System is in a galaxy we call the Milky Way.

gas

A gas is a substance with no fixed shape or volume. Most gases are invisible, but some smell strongly, for example chlorine.

 volume

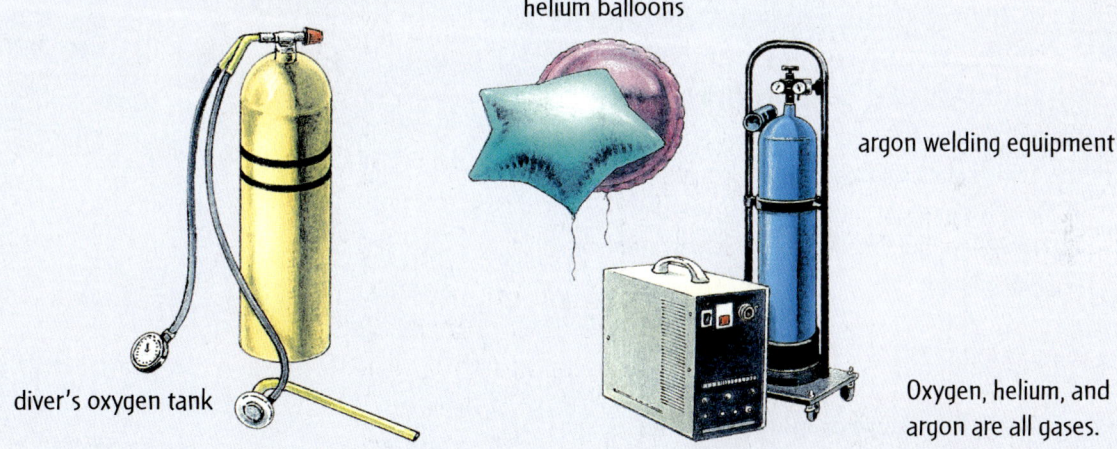

helium balloons

argon welding equipment

diver's oxygen tank

Oxygen, helium, and argon are all gases.

gastropod

A gastropod is an animal that moves around on a single fleshy foot. The name means 'stomach foot'. Gastropods are molluscs.

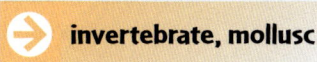 invertebrate, mollusc

Snails are gastropods.

gauge (rhymes with 'cage')

A gauge is a standard measuring scale.

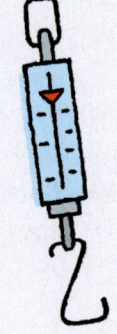

These are both types of gauge.

gear

A gear is a toothed wheel. Two gears meshed together can alter the speed and direction of a turning movement.

The two gear wheels turn opposite ways.

gender

A living thing is usually either male or female gender. Some animals are hermaphrodites.

Some plants, like maize, have separate male and female sexual parts. Others, like the rose, have both male and female parts in the same flower.

 female, hermaphrodite, male

maize   rose flower

gene

Genes are short lengths of chromosomes. They are responsible for eye colour, hair colour, blood type, and inherited disease.

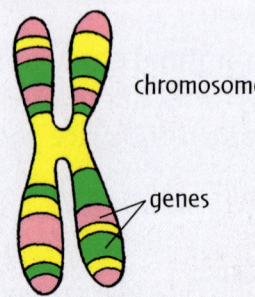

chromosome

genes

chromosome, DNA, reproduction

People pass on their genes when they reproduce.

generator

Generators are devices that produce electricity.

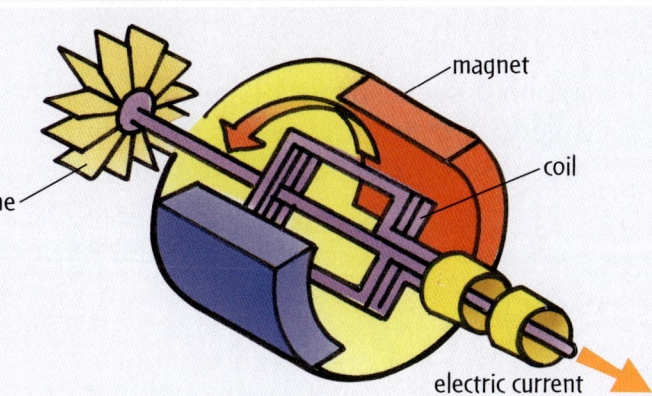

magnet

coil

turbine

electric current

Turning the blades of the turbine turns a coil of wire between two magnets. This produces electricity.

genitals

The word genitals refers to the external sexual organs of animals.

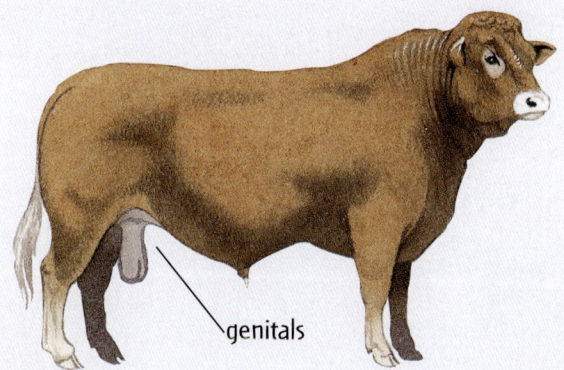

genitals

➡ **penis, sexual intercourse, testicle, vagina**

geology

Geology is the study of rocks.

➡ **rock**

A geologist is someone who studies geology.

germ

Germs are micro-organisms that can infect us and cause disease.

➡ **bacterium, fungus, micro-organism, virus**

germinate

When a seed sprouts it germinates. A seed needs warmth and water to germinate. Light is not needed to make most seeds start growing.

 seed

A sunflower germinating.

gestation

Gestation is the period that a fetus stays in its mother's body. This word applies only to mammals.

 fetus, mammal

Different mammals have different gestation periods.

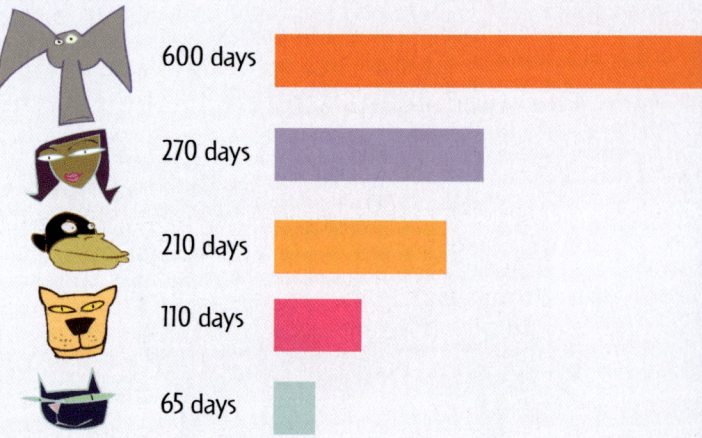

600 days

270 days

210 days

110 days

65 days

gill

Animals that live all their lives in water breathe using gills.

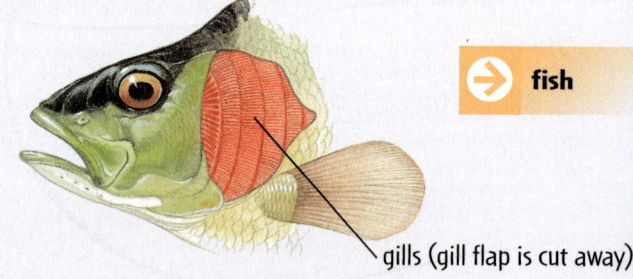

fish

Gill flaps cover a fish's gills.

gills (gill flap is cut away)

glass

Glass is a hard, shiny, brittle material that is usually transparent. It is made by melting sand with other chemicals.

 brittle, chemical, transparent

Glassblowers blow hot glass into shapes such as bottles and vases.

global warming

The Earth's climate is warming. Scientists think it is happening because we burn fuel. The gases produced cause a greenhouse effect.

 burn, carbon dioxide, fossil fuel, gas

As the Earth warms up, the ice at the North and South Poles begins to melt and break up.

GM food

GM is short for genetic modification. This involves changing the genes in the cells of a living thing. Scientists have developed GM food plants that grow bigger or resist disease.

 cell, DNA, nucleus

Some people think GM crops will be very useful. Others think they are dangerous.

gold

Gold is a yellow metal that is soft and easily shaped. It is a very dense material.

 **density, material, metal**

This ancient helmet is made of solid gold.

graph

Graphs are diagrams that help show information.

bar graph showing
favourite foods in our class

number of children

pie chart showing
proportion of animals on the farm

graphite

Pencil leads are made from graphite.
It is a form of carbon.

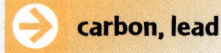 carbon, lead

grass

Grasses are flowering
plants with long thin
leaves. Bamboo, wheat,
maize, and oats are all
types of grass.

All grasses are pollinated by the wind.

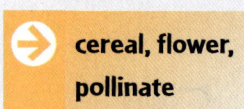 cereal, flower,
pollinate

gravity

The force that attracts objects to the Earth is called gravity.

When an apple falls from a tree it is pulled down by gravity.

 Earth, force

greenhouse effect

The way that the Earth's atmosphere traps heat from the Sun is called the greenhouse effect.

some heat is absorbed by gases in the atmosphere

 atmosphere, ozone

sunlight

some heat is radiated back into space

grub

Grub is another word for the larva of an insect.

 insect, larva

gut

The gut is another word for the intestines.

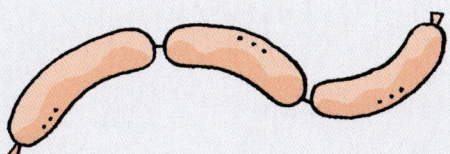 **bowel, intestine**

In the past pigs' guts were used to make sausage skins.

Hh

habitat

The place where an animal or plant lives is its habitat.

Wildebeest, zebra, and antelope live in the savannah grasslands.

 adapted, environment

heart

The heart is a pump that pushes blood round the body.

heart

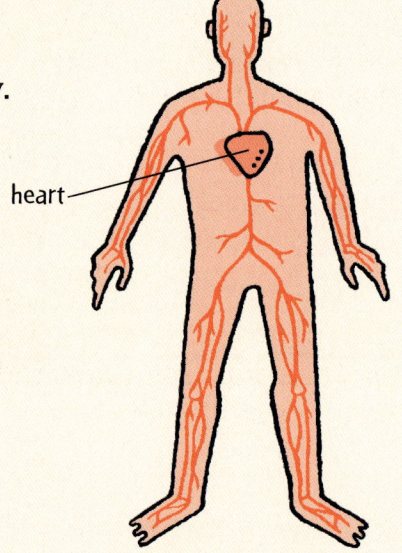

**artery,
blood,
capillary,
vein**

heat

Heat is a form of energy. It can be measured using a thermometer.

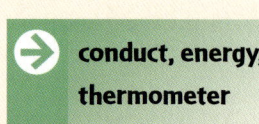 **conduct, energy,
thermometer**

metal spoon

Heat travels easily through metals.

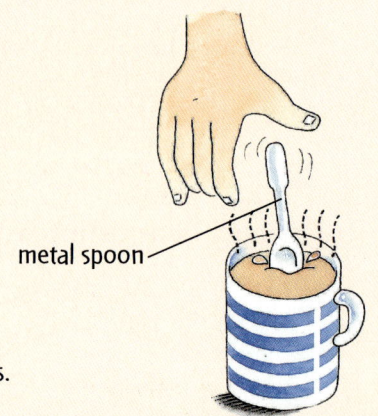

herbivore

Animals that only eat plants are herbivores. They are the second link in many food chains.

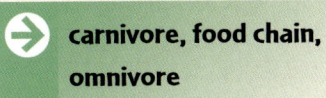 carnivore, food chain, omnivore

Deer are herbivores.

heredity

Heredity is the process that makes living things grow to look like their parents. People inherit the way they look from their mother and father.

 chromosome, gene

hermaphrodite

A living thing that has both male and female sex organs is a hermaphrodite.

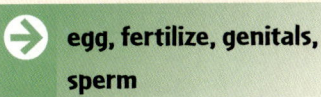 egg, fertilize, genitals, sperm

Earthworms are hermaphrodites but they cannot fertilize their own eggs. They give sperm to each other when they mate.

heroin

Heroin is a dangerous drug made from certain types of poppy.

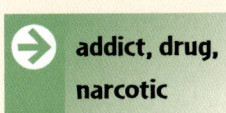 addict, drug, narcotic

Some heroin users inject. Others smoke it.

honey

Bees make honey from the nectar they collect from flowers. Bees feed honey to their growing larvae.

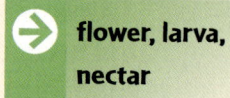
→ flower, larva, nectar

Bees store honey in a honeycomb.

hot air balloon

Hot air balloons have a gas heater to warm the air in the envelope. This makes the air inside the envelope lighter. Upthrust from the air makes the balloon rise.

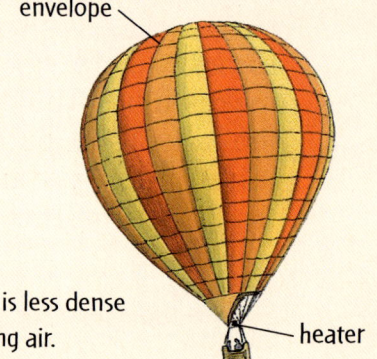
envelope

heater

→ air, gas, gravity, upthrust

The hot air in the balloon is less dense than the cooler surrounding air.

human

Human beings are people. You are a human being.

How humans grow.

young adults   teenager   child   toddler   baby

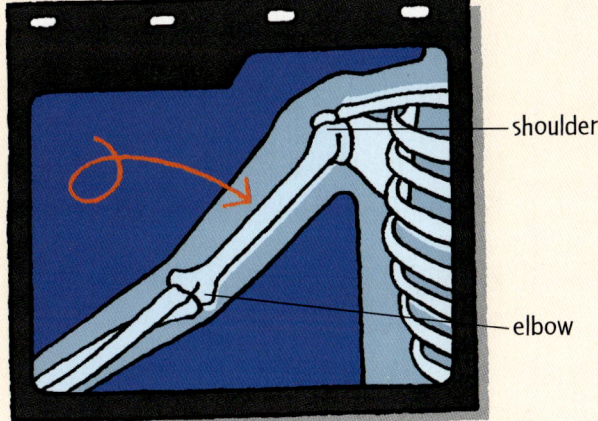

humerus

The bone connecting your elbow and your shoulder is called the humerus.

shoulder

elbow

 bone

humus

Humus is plant remains that have rotted away and mixed with the top part of the soil.

Humus enriches the soil.

much humus

less humus

rock

 decay, rot, soil

hydrogen

Hydrogen is a gas that burns very easily. Water is made by burning hydrogen.

Hydrogen is used as a fuel in rockets.

 gas, water

Ii

ice

Ice is the solid form of water.
Ice forms when water freezes.

 **freeze, water**

igneous rock

Igneous rocks form when hot, liquid rock from deep in the Earth cools and becomes solid.

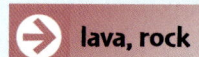 **lava, rock**

When lava from a volcano cools, it forms igneous rock.

lava

cooled igneous rocks

image

An image is a picture formed by a lens.

 lens, light

The photographer has taken an image of a cat.

immunize

When people and animals are immunized they are injected with dead germs. This helps the body protect itself against a real virus or bacteria attack.

 bacterium, germ, virus

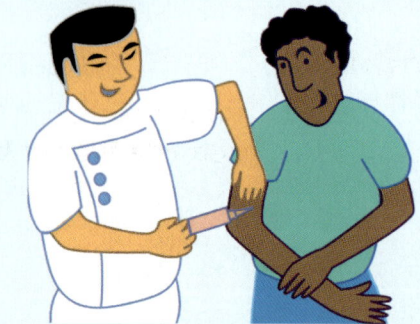

impermeable

Water cannot go through impermeable materials.

 permeable, water

incubate

When birds incubate eggs, they sit on them to keep them warm until their chicks hatch. Micro-organisms grow faster if they are kept warm in an incubator.

 egg, micro-organism

Some tiny babies need to be kept warm in an incubator.

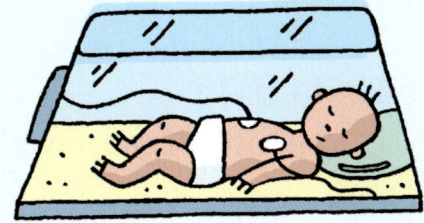

indigenous

If a plant or animal is indigenous to a place, it lives naturally there. Indigenous is the opposite of alien.

 alien

The kangaroo is indigenous to Australia.

infect

Germs infect a person when they get inside their body. Once they are there they can multiply.

 AIDS, germ

When you sneeze, germs shoot out of your mouth and nose.

inflammable

Inflammable materials burn very easily. Hydrogen is a highly inflammable gas.

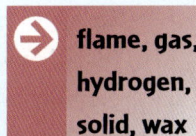 flame, gas, hydrogen, solid, wax

Candles are made from inflammable wax.

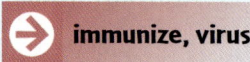

influenza

Influenza is an infection caused by a virus. It is known as flu for short.

→ **immunize, virus**

Flu makes anyone feel miserable but it can be especially dangerous to old people.

infra-red

Infra-red is energy which we feel as heat.

→ **energy**

The television remote control works using infra-red.

inoculate

See immunize.

inorganic

Inorganic things do not come from living organisms. Rocks and metal are inorganic.

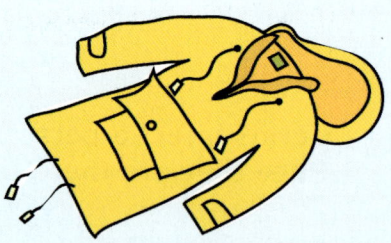

→ **nylon, organic**

Nylon is inorganic.

insect

An insect is an animal that has three parts to its body. It also has six legs.

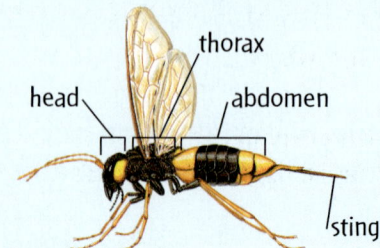

thorax

head

abdomen

sting

→ **abdomen, beetle, thorax**

Most insects have wings, but only wasps and bees have a sting.

insoluble

Solids that do not dissolve in a liquid are insoluble.

liquid, solid, soluble, solute, solution, solvent

Flour is insoluble in water.

instinct

Animals know how to do some things by instinct. They don't have to be taught.

These baby turtles act on instinct when they run towards the sea.

insulate (electricity)

An electrical insulator does not allow electricity to pass through it.

The plastic around the wire is a good insulator.

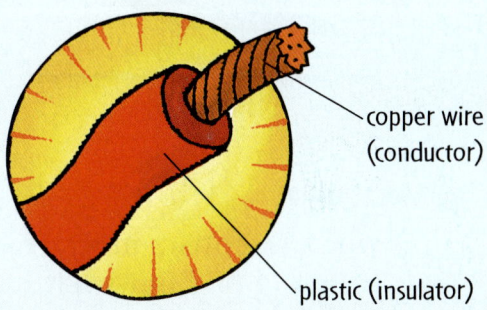

copper wire (conductor)

plastic (insulator)

conduct (electricity)

insulate (heat)

Materials that insulate heat stop it from travelling from hot to cooler places.

The oven gloves act as insulators to keep the heat from the oven tray burning the man's hands.

fat, feather

intestine

After food has been in the stomach it passes through the intestines. This is where most digestion happens.

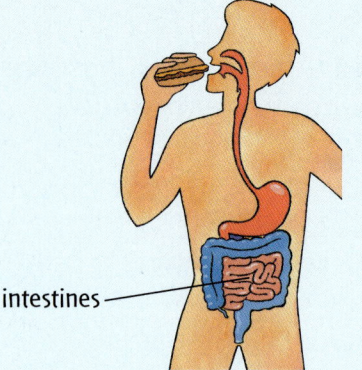

intestines

→ **digest, gut, stomach**

invertebrate

Animals that do not have backbones are invertebrates.

→ **insect, spine, vertebrate**

sea anemone

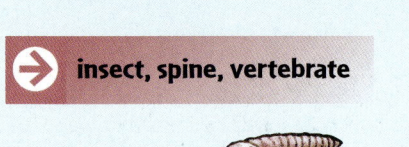

butterfly

jellyfish

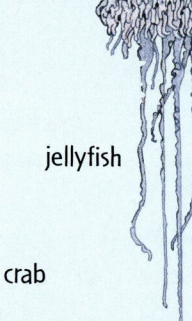

millipede

earthworm

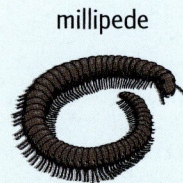

crab

All these animals are invertebrates.

investigate

When scientists investigate they are trying to find out what happens when something is changed.

→ **experiment**

These children are investigating what happens if you change the size of a parachute.

iris

The iris is the coloured part of the eye around the pupil.

iris

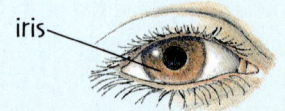

→ **eye, pupil**

In bright light the iris spreads out to make the pupil smaller. This protects the eye from the bright light.

iron

Iron is a metal. It is very strong. When small amounts of carbon and other metals are added iron becomes steel.

iron ore, the type of rock we get iron from

We get iron by heating iron ore in a blast furnace.

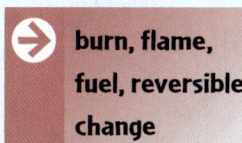
blast furnace

→ carbon, rust, steel

irreversible change

Changes that are irreversible can't be undone. When a piece of wood is burnt it changes irreversibly.

→ burn, flame, fuel, reversible change

Jj

joint

The place where two bones meet is a joint. There are three sorts of joint.

→ bone

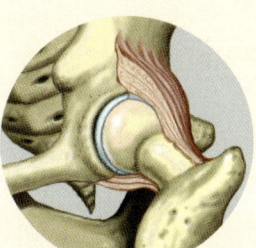
ball-and-socket or swivel joint (hip)

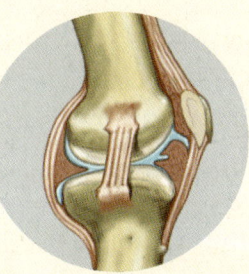
hinge joint (knee)

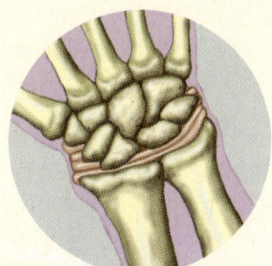
sliding joint (wrist)

Kk

kidney

Kidneys filter the blood. They remove unwanted chemicals. These are diluted with water to make urine.

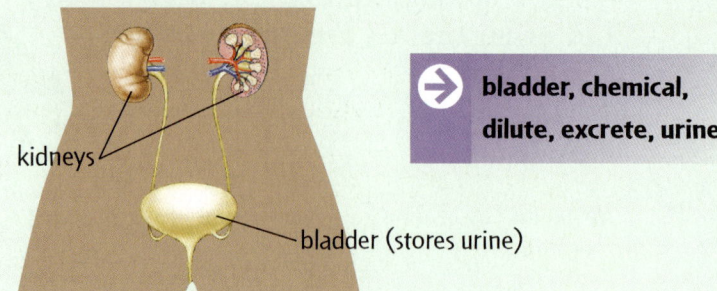

kidneys

bladder (stores urine)

→ bladder, chemical, dilute, excrete, urine

kilogram

The kilogram is the unit we use to measure mass.

→ mass

One litre of water has a mass of 1 kilogram.

kilojoule

The amount of food energy is measured in kilojoules. The joule is a measure of work or energy. There are 1000 joules in a kilojoule.

→ calorie, energy, food, work

kJ is the abbreviation of kilojoules.

Children of ten years old need approximately 10 000 kilojoules of food energy each day.

kinetic energy

Kinetic energy is another word for movement energy. Light objects moving slowly have very little kinetic energy. Heavy, fast moving objects have lots.

The cyclist has lots of kinetic energy. The car is not moving, so it has no kinetic energy.

Ll

larva (plural larvae)

A larva is in the caterpillar stage of an insect. Larvae of flies are called maggots.

→ caterpillar, insect, life cycle, maggot, pupa

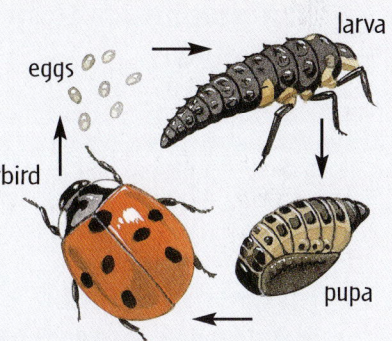

Eggs hatch into larvae.
Larvae form pupae.
Pupae form into adults.

laser

Lasers produce very concentrated light beams. Some are used in delicate surgery on eyes. Powerful lasers can even cut through metal.

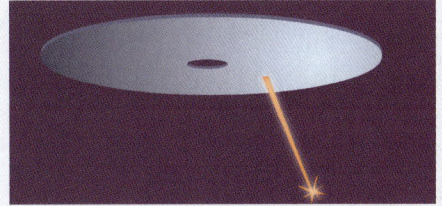

CD players use lasers to read CDs.

lava

Lava is molten rock that flows from volcanoes.

→ freeze, igneous, liquid, magma, solid, volcano

lead (metal)

Lead is a soft, dense, grey metal. It makes marks on paper.

→ density, metal

The pieces of glass in this church window are held together with strips of lead.

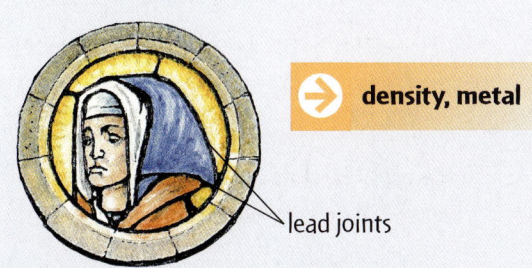

lead joints

lead (pencil)

Pencil lead is made from a mixture of graphite (a form of carbon) and dry clay.

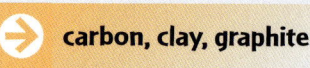
carbon, clay, graphite

leaf

Plants make food in their leaves using the process of photosynthesis.

We eat some kinds of leaves.

 food, photosynthesis

parsley

cabbage

tea

lens

A lens is a piece of glass or plastic with two curved surfaces. Lenses are used in microscopes, telescopes, and cameras.

 concave, convex, image, light

lever

A lever is a long rod that pivots. A small force on the long end of the rod makes a bigger force on the short end.

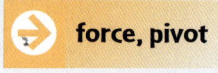 force, pivot

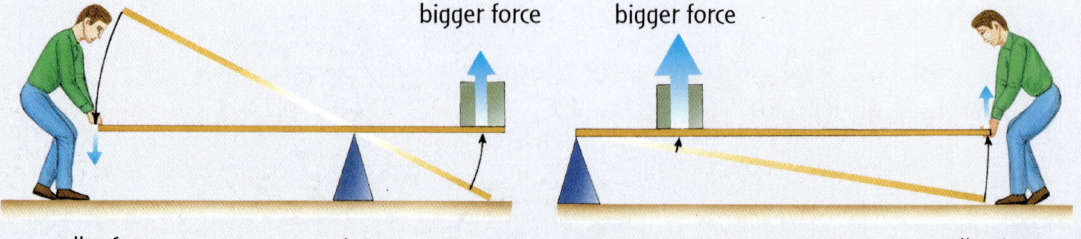

bigger force   bigger force

smaller force   pivot   smaller force

lice

Lice are the blood-sucking insects that sometimes live on people's skin. People infected with large numbers of lice feel 'lousy'.

You can tell a louse is an insect because it has six legs.

infect, insect

life cycle

A life cycle shows the way in which a living thing changes as it grows. It also describes the way in which reproduction takes place.

Insects have one of two types of life cycle.

 insect, larva, reproduction

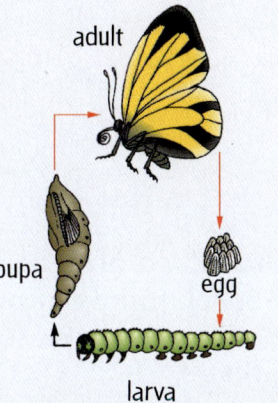
adult
pupa
egg
larva

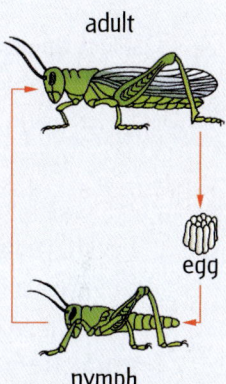
adult
egg
nymph

life processes

The mark of all living things is that they carry out these processes:

a. move (plants move but it is difficult to see)
b. reproduce
c. grow
d. respond to their environment
e. exchange gases. We breathe out carbon dioxide. Plants give off oxygen during the day and carbon dioxide at night.
f. feed
g. excrete

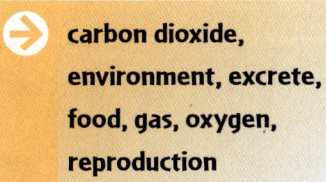 carbon dioxide, environment, excrete, food, gas, oxygen, reproduction

a.
b.
c.

d.

e.
f.
g.

light

Light is a form of energy we can detect with our eyes. Light can be split into the colours of the spectrum.

colour, energy, rainbow, spectrum

Where an object blocks the light, you get a shadow.

lightning

Lightning is the flash of light caused when an electrical spark jumps between clouds. The spark can also jump between a cloud and the ground.

During thunderstorms, lightning can strike buildings, trees, or animals.

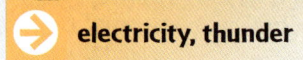

electricity, thunder

limb

A limb is a part of the body that sticks out. Legs, arms, and wings are all limbs.

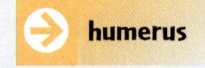

humerus

leg of a frog

wing of an insect

wing of a bird

arm of an ape

liquid

Liquids flow and take the shape of their container.

 fluid, gas, solid

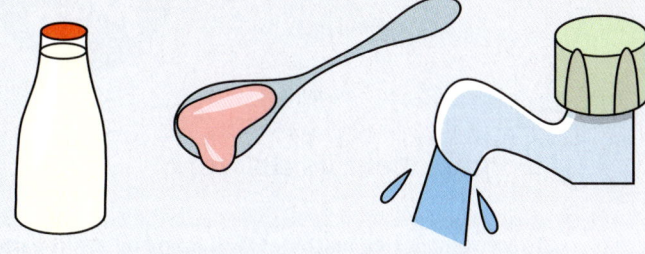

In a liquid the particles flow over each other.

liver

The liver is one of the main organs of the body. It is an energy store and the body's main producer of chemicals.

 chemical, energy, organ

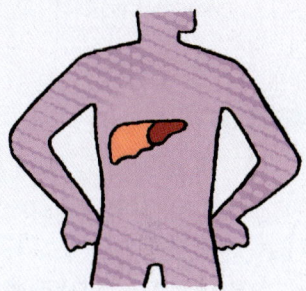

lunar

Anything to do with the Moon is called lunar. The lunar month is approximately 28 days long.

 eclipse

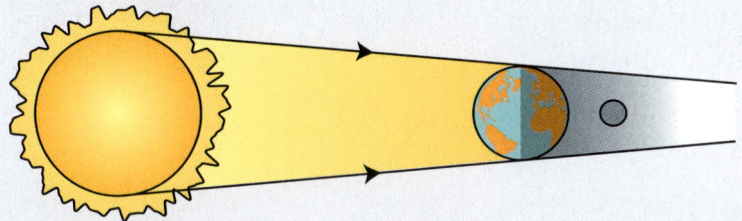

In a lunar eclipse the shadow of the Earth stops the Sun's light from hitting the full Moon.

lung

The lungs are organs that take in oxygen from the air and excrete carbon dioxide from the body.

Inside the lungs are branching air tubes called bronchioles.

 air, carbon dioxide, excrete, oxygen

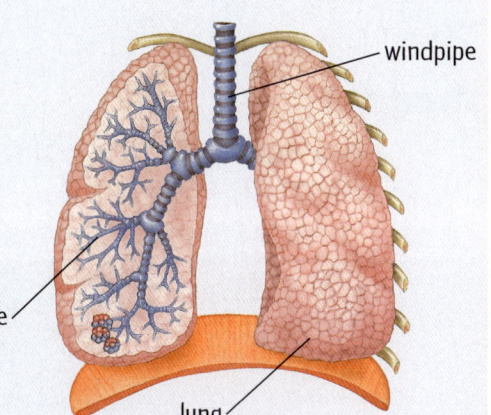

windpipe

bronchiole

lung

Mm

machine

Machines help us do work.

Cars are complicated machines with many different parts. They help us to move about quickly.

 gear, lever, work

maggot

A maggot is a larva. There are many types of maggot.

Maggots will turn into pupae then into adult flies.

larva, pupa

magma

Magma is molten rock that is deep underground. It forms lava when it flows from a volcano.

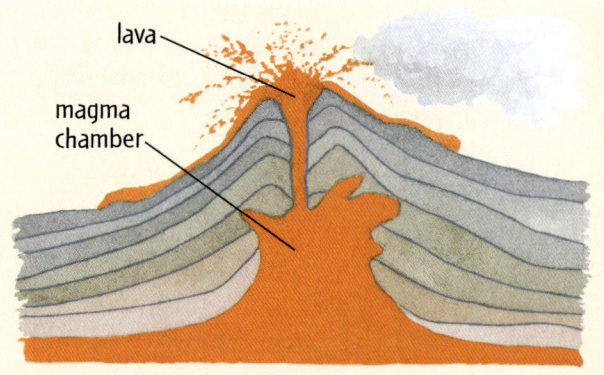

lava

magma chamber

 igneous, lava, volcano

magnet

A magnet is a piece of iron or steel that exerts a magnetic force.

 magnetism

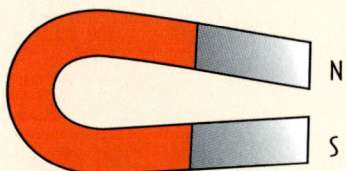

N

S

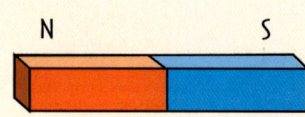

N   S

magnetic pole

All magnets have a north and a south pole. A north pole and a south pole attract each other. Two north poles, or two south poles, repel each other.

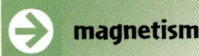

→ magnetism

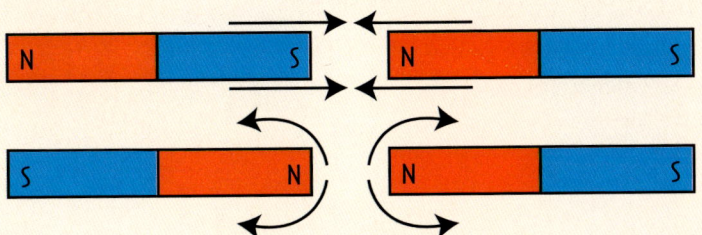

magnetism

Magnetism is an invisible force that attracts the metals iron, steel, cobalt, and nickel.

→ force, iron, steel

These magnets attract steel paper clips.

magnify

When an object is magnified it is made larger.

The magnifying glass makes the picture look larger.

→ lens, microscope

male

Males are the animal sex that produces sperm. The male parts of a flower produce pollen.

→ anther, flower, pollen, semen, sperm, testicle

mammal

Mammals are a type of animal. Their skin is usually hairy. They feed their young on milk and most give birth to live young.

chipmunk

orang-utan

platypus

rhinoceros

stoat

→ **animal, mammal**

All these animals are mammals.

manufactured

Manufactured objects and materials are those made by people.

This chair is being made by hand, but many manufactured goods are made in factories.

→ **material, natural, plastic**

mass

Mass is the amount of a substance. Mass is measured in grams and kilograms. Compare this with weight.

→ **density, kilogram, weight**

The mass of something does not change, wherever you measure it.

material

Objects are made from a material.

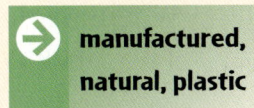

manufactured, natural, plastic

made from cotton or wool

made from rubber

made from steel

matter

Matter is the scientific word for the stuff that all things are made of. The Sun, Moon, sand, air, plants, and animals are all made of matter.

a sunflower

maximum

The biggest amount is the maximum.

minimum

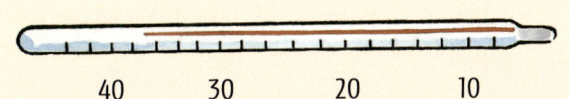

The maximum temperature ever in Britain was 37 °C.

medicine

Medicines are chemicals we take to make us feel better or to cure a disease.

Antibiotics are medicines that kill bacteria.

antibiotic, chemical, disease

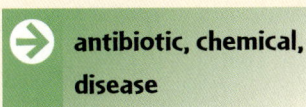

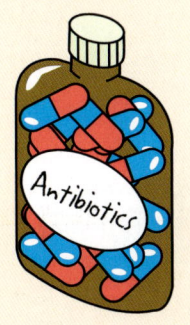

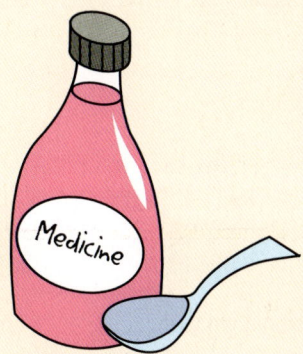

melt

When a solid melts it changes into a liquid.
This usually happens when the solid is heated.

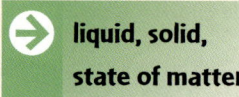 liquid, solid,
state of matter

A lolly left out of the freezer will melt.

menstruation

Women lose a small amount of blood each month through menstruation. The blood carries the unfertilized egg out of the womb and vagina.

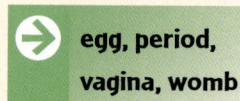 egg, period,
vagina, womb

tampon

sanitary towel

Women use tampons or sanitary towels to soak up the small amount of blood.

mercury

Mercury is a silvery metal. It is liquid at room temperature. Mercury is used in thermometers.

Mercury rises up a thermometer as it heats up.

 liquid, thermometer

metal

Metals are materials that conduct electricity and heat.

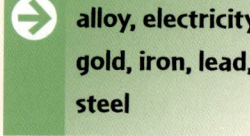 alloy, electricity,
gold, iron, lead,
steel

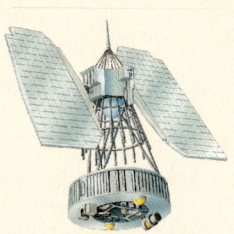

aluminium (satellite)

gold (jewellery)

copper (wire)

steel (tools)

metamorphic rock

Metamorphic rocks are igneous or sedimentary rocks that have been changed by heat or compression.

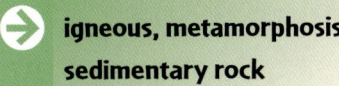
→ igneous, metamorphosis, sedimentary rock

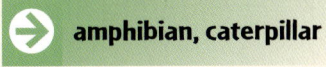
metamorphic rock

metamorphosis

A metamorphosis is a major change from one form to another.

→ amphibian, caterpillar

A tadpole metamorphoses into a frog.

meteor

A meteor is a streak of light across the night sky. This happens when a piece of rock from space burns up in the atmosphere.

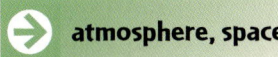
→ atmosphere, space

Meteors often come in showers when the Earth passes through dust in space.

micro-organism

Micro-organisms are tiny living creatures. Most can only be seen through a microscope. Bacteria, fungi, and viruses are all examples of micro-organisms.

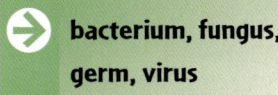
→ bacterium, fungus, germ, virus

Yeast is a fungus used in cookery. Yeast makes bread rise.

microscope

Microscopes are used to magnify tiny objects.

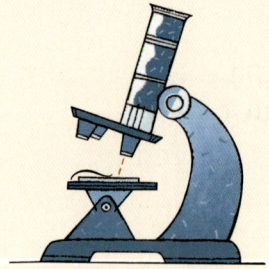

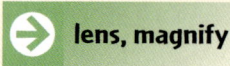
lens, magnify

You can see things as small as bacteria through a good microscope.

midnight

Midnight is twelve o'clock at night.

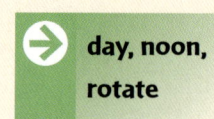
day, noon, rotate

Midnight and midday are both twelve o'clock.

midsummer

Midsummer is the time of the year when the Sun is at its highest in the sky, and we have the longest day. Midsummer is another word for summer solstice.

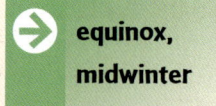
equinox, midwinter

The longest day in the northern hemisphere is 21st June and in the southern hemisphere is about 21st December.

midwinter

Midwinter is the time of the year when the Sun is at its lowest in the sky, and we have the shortest day. Midwinter is another word for winter solstice.

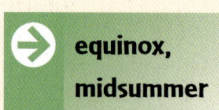
equinox, midsummer

The shortest day in the northern hemisphere is 21st December and in the southern hemisphere is about 21st June.

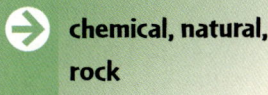

mineral

A mineral is a chemical that occurs naturally.
It can be dug out of the ground.

→ chemical, natural, rock

Coal, salt, and diamonds are all minerals.

minimum

The smallest amount of something is the minimum.

→ maximum, temperature

The minimum temperature ever recorded was –89°C.

mirror

A mirror is a sheet of glass or metal.
An image is reflected off the mirror.

→ concave, convex, image, reflect

molecule

A molecule is a tiny particle. It is a group of atoms that are strongly attracted to each other.

Water molecules are made from two hydrogen atoms and one oxygen atom.

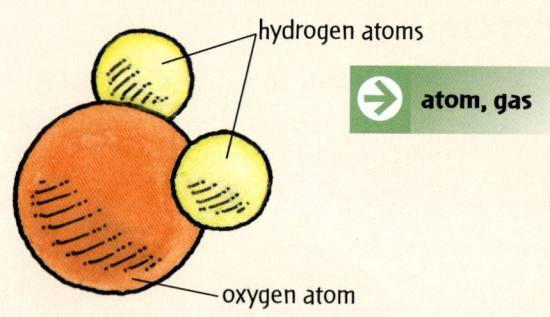

hydrogen atoms

oxygen atom

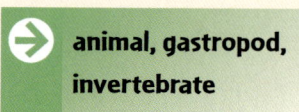

→ atom, gas

mollusc

Molluscs are a type of animal with a soft body. Their body is not divided into segments. They usually have a shell.

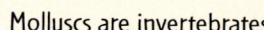

→ animal, gastropod, invertebrate

blue-ringed octopus   oyster   garden snail

Molluscs are invertebrates.

momentum

Objects that are moving have momentum. Moving objects need another force to slow or stop them. Heavy objects have more momentum than light objects travelling at the same speed.

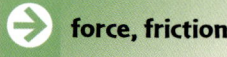

→ force, friction

Fast – lots of momentum: difficult to stop.

Slow – little momentum: easy to stop.

Moon

The Moon is a satellite of the Earth. It orbits the Earth once every 28 days. It is lit by the Sun.

Moon's orbit
last quarter
Earth
new Moon
full Moon
first quarter

new Moon   first quarter   full Moon   last quarter

→ lunar, orbit, reflect, satellite

When the Moon is full we see all of one side. At the new Moon we cannot see any part of it.

moss

Mosses are small plants that usually grow in wet places. Mosses do not flower, they reproduce using spores.

→ plant, reproduction, spore

mould

A fungus that forms a woolly coating on food, wood, or other organic matter is called mould.

→ fungus

mucus

Mucus is a sticky, slimy substance that protects parts of our body. The insides of our lungs are coated with mucus. Slugs and snails use mucus to help them slide along the ground.

→ lungs

When you sneeze, droplets of mucus shoot out of your nose.

muscle

Muscles are the tissues which pull our skeleton so we can move. The heart is also a muscle.

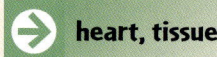 heart, tissue

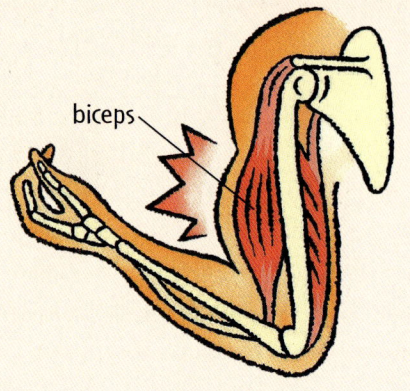

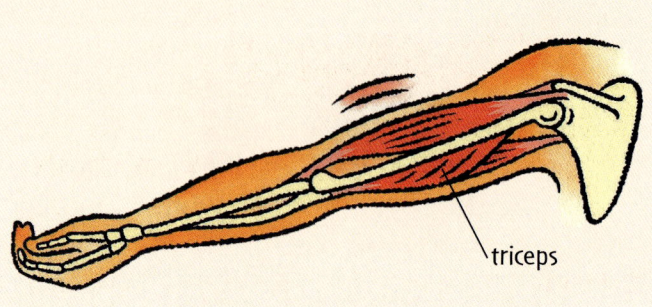

The biceps muscle makes the arm bend.

The triceps muscle straightens the arm.

mushroom

Mushrooms are a sort of fungus. Many people eat them.

 fungus

Some mushrooms are good to eat, but many wild mushrooms are poisonous.

myriapod

Animals with many legs are members of the myriapod group.

arthropod, gastropod

All myriapods are part of the arthropod group.

centipede

millipede

Nn

narcotic

A drug that makes people sleepy is called a narcotic.

 drug, heroin, medicine

Narcotic medicines can be dangerous. They can only be prescribed by doctors.

natural

A natural object or material has not been interfered with in any way by people.

 manufactured, material

nectar

The sweet sticky liquid inside a flower is nectar. It attracts bees, which turn the nectar into honey.

 flower, honey

nerve

Nerves are the long thin tissues that send messages around our body.

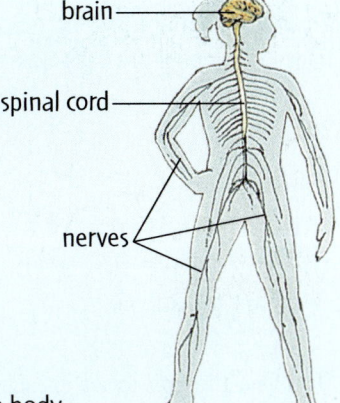

brain

spinal cord

nerves

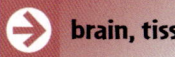 brain, tissue

Nerves run to all parts of the body.

newton

The unit for measuring force is the newton.

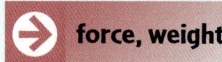
force, weight

The pull of gravity on an average size apple is one newton.

nicotine

Nicotine is the drug that makes tobacco addictive.

Nicotine is very addictive. Most smokers want to stop but find it difficult to do so.

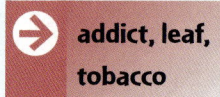
addict, leaf, tobacco

night

The time of day when our part of the Earth is facing away from the Sun is night.

day, orbit

It is night on this side of the Earth.

nitrogen

Nitrogen is the most common gas in the atmosphere.

Crisps keep better if there is no oxygen in the bag, so crisp bags are filled with nitrogen.

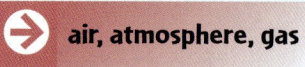
air, atmosphere, gas

nocturnal

Animals that are awake during the night are nocturnal.

Owls have big eyes to see at night. Many bats use sound echoes to find their way in the dark.

owl

bat

noon

Noon is at twelve o'clock midday. The Sun is at its highest in the sky at noon.

 day

nuclear power

In a nuclear power station, heat is produced when an atom's nucleus is broken apart. The heat is used to make steam, which drives the electricity generator.

The waste products of nuclear power are dangerous for many years.

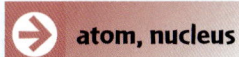 atom, nucleus

nucleus (plural nuclei)

1. There is a nucleus at the centre of an atom.

2. A cell's nucleus controls the way it works.

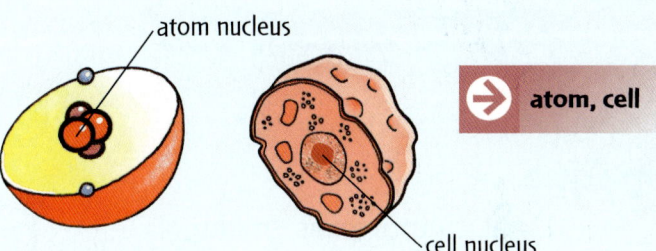

atom nucleus

cell nucleus

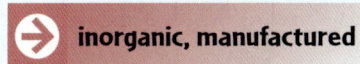 atom, cell

nylon

Nylon is a type of plastic that can be made into strong threads.

inorganic, manufactured

NYLON BRISTLES

Nylon has many uses.

Oo

oil

Oil is a black sticky liquid that is trapped in rocks underground. It is used to make plastics, petrol, wax, and many other chemicals.

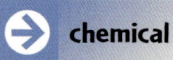
chemical

Another thing made from oil is oil!

omnivore

Animals that eat both vegetation and other animals are omnivores.

Herring gulls are omnivores. They will eat almost anything.

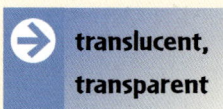
animal, carnivore, herbivore

opaque

Light cannot pass through objects that are opaque.

The glass is transparent but the boy is opaque.

translucent, transparent

optical fibre

Glass can be made into very thin fibres. These are called optical fibres because light can travel down them.

light

Many telephone calls travel through optical fibres.

orbit

Objects that circle other objects are in orbit around them.

Satellites orbit the Earth.

ore

Ore is a mixture of rock and metal. It is dug out of the ground.

Iron ore being loaded into a dumper truck.

 metal, mineral

organ

Organs are parts of the body that do a particular job.

 brain, heart, kidney, liver, lungs, stomach

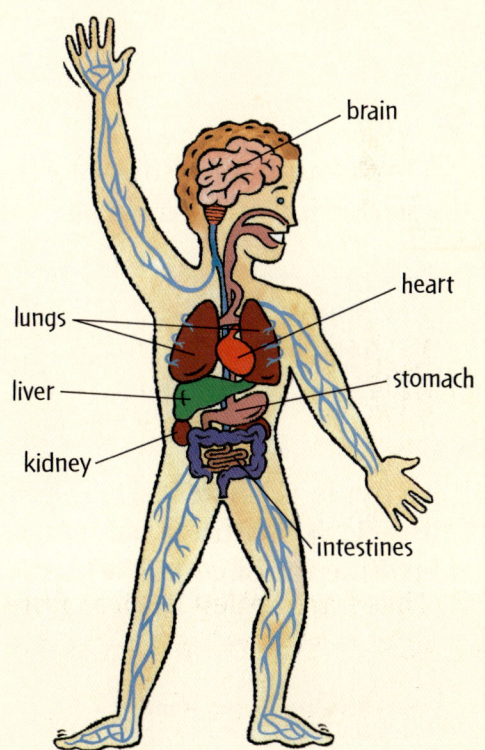

These are all organs.

organic matter

Organic matter comes from plants and animals. All organic matter is alive, or was once alive. The opposite of organic is inorganic.

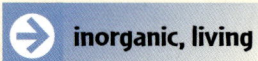 inorganic, living

Trees and rotten wood are organic matter.

organism

All living things are organisms.

chimpanzee (mammal)

swallow (bird)

tulip (plant)

shark (fish)

fly agaric (fungus)

ovary

The ovary is the part of a female animal or flower where eggs are produced.

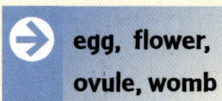 egg, flower, ovule, womb

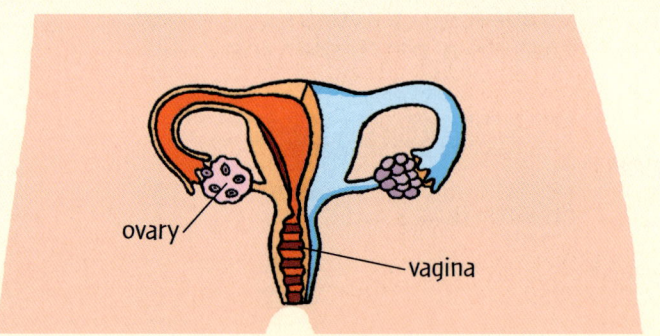

ovary

vagina

ovule

An ovule is an unfertilized seed in a flower. After it has been fertilized it becomes a seed.

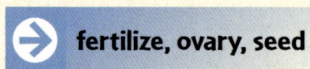 fertilize, ovary, seed

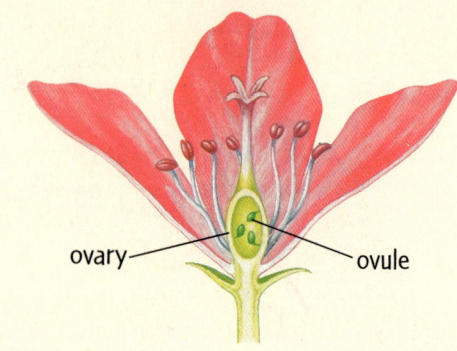

ovary

ovule

ovum (plural ova)

An ovum is an unfertilized animal egg cell.

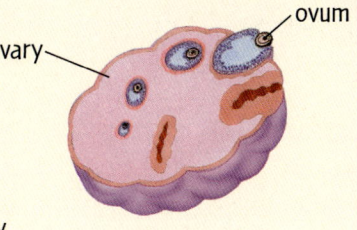

Ova grow inside the ovary.

→ cell, sperm, uterus, womb

oxide

An oxide is a compound in which oxygen is combined with another chemical.

→ compound, iron, oxygen, rust

Rusty iron is iron oxide.

oxygen

Oxygen is a gas. It makes up about a fifth of the atmosphere. It is vital for living things.

→ atmosphere, compound, gas, hydrogen

Water is a compound of oxygen and hydrogen.

ozone

Ozone is a special type of oxygen. The ozone layer of the atmosphere protects the Earth from dangerous rays from the Sun.

→ atmosphere, greenhouse effect

stratosphere

ionosphere

ozone

Pp

parallel circuit

In a parallel circuit electricity can take more than one path round a circuit.

 electricity, series circuit

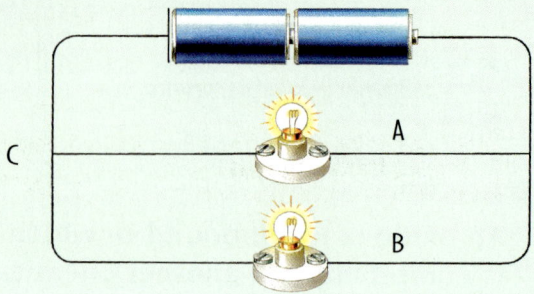

Electricity can travel though A or B. It meets up again at C.

parasite

A parasite is a type of plant or animal that gets all its food from another plant or animal.

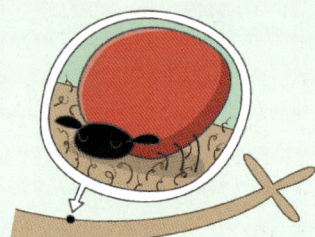

A tick is a parasite that lives by sucking blood from another animal.

peat

Peat is a crumbly brown material made from partly decayed vegetation. Dried peat can be used as a fuel.

 decay, rot

Some people grow tomatoes in bags of peat.

pendulum

A pendulum is a swinging weight on the end of a piece of string. Only the length of the string affects how fast the pendulum swings, not how big the swing is.

In some old clocks, a pendulum is used to help keep the clock running on time.

penicillin

Penicillin is an antibiotic made from a fungus.

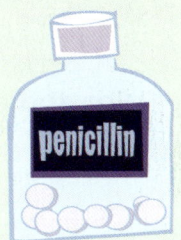

 antibiotic, fungus

Penicillin kills many of the bacteria that make cuts go septic.

penis

The penis is the male organ through which urine and sperm are released.

 **genitals, male, organ, sperm, urine**

period

Women release an egg each month, and if it is not fertilized, they menstruate. The cycle is called a period. Menstruation is called 'having a period'.

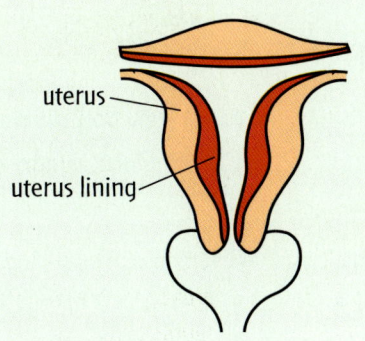

uterus

uterus lining

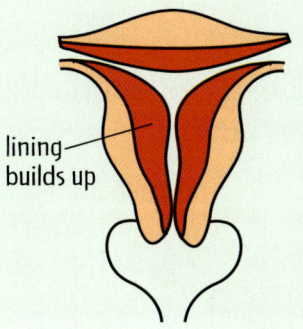

lining builds up

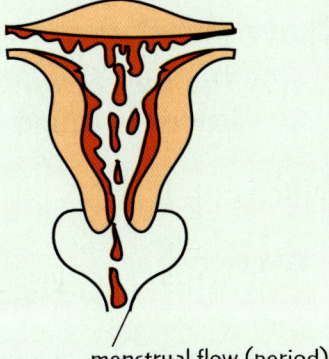

menstrual flow (period)

 egg, menstruation, vagina

periscope

A periscope is a device for seeing around corners, or above the water surface from underwater.

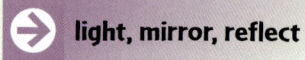 light, mirror, reflect

People in submarines use a periscope so they can see above the surface of the water.

permeable

Water can go through permeable materials.

 impermeable

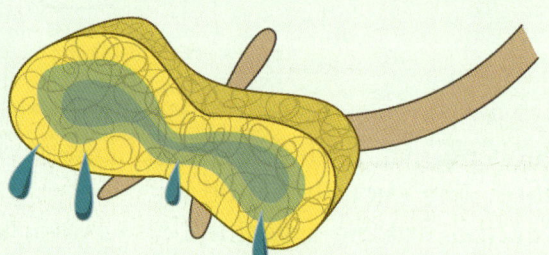

A natural sponge is permeable.

photosynthesis

The way in which plants make food in their leaves is called photosynthesis.

carbon dioxide, plant, sugar, water

oxygen (waste product)

water from soil

sugar to rest of plant   carbon dioxide

The leaf takes in water from the roots and carbon dioxide from the air to make sugar. It needs energy from light to make this happen.

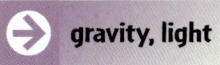

physics

Physics is the study of the non-living world. Physicists investigate atoms and stars. They look at how things move, and study different kinds of energy, such as light and magnetism.

gravity, light

Physicists ask questions about what causes a rainbow. They want to know why objects fall to the ground.

pitch

Pitch is a measure of how high or low sound is.

sound

high-pitched

low-pitched

High-pitched sounds are screechy. Low-pitched sounds are growly.

pivot

The place where a lever turns is called the pivot.

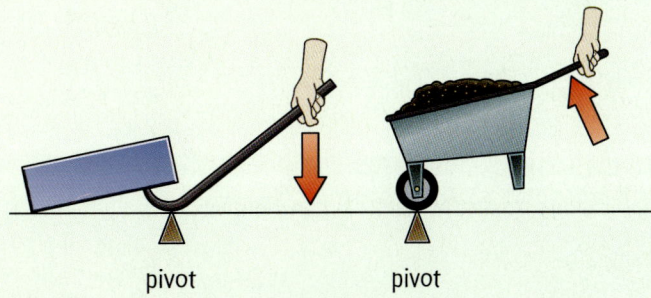

pivot   pivot

lever

109

placenta

The organ that feeds a baby in the womb is the placenta.

womb

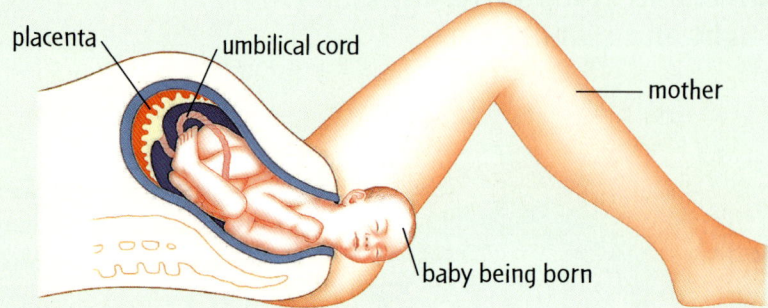

placenta   umbilical cord

mother

baby being born

You were attached to your mother's placenta through the umbilical cord. It was attached where your belly button is now.

planet

The planets of the Solar System are large objects made of rock or gas. They all orbit the Sun.

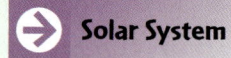
Solar System

Sun

Neptune

Earth Mars

Venus

Mercury

Jupiter

Saturn

Uranus

Pluto

plankton

Plankton are very tiny animals and plants that live in water. Other water creatures rely on plankton for food.

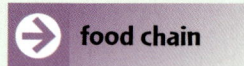
food chain

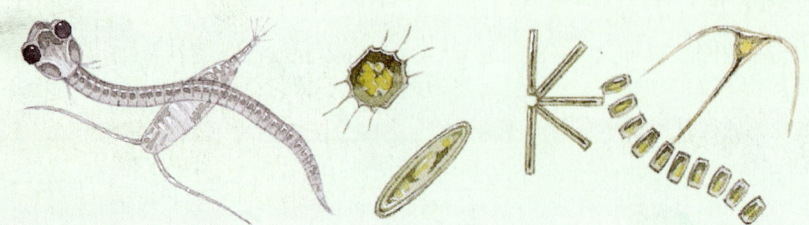

Plankton are the base of many food chains.

plant

Plants are living things that use the Sun's light to make food.

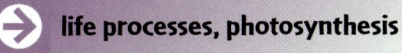 **life processes, photosynthesis**

moss   fern   Scots pine (conifer)   sunflower (flowering plant)

plastic

Plastic is a material that can easily be moulded when warm.

Plastic is used to make many things.

 manufactured, oil

pneumonia

Pneumonia is an infection of the lungs. It killed many people before antibiotics were invented.

In pneumonia some of the air sacs of the lung fill with liquid.

 antibiotic, bacterium, lung

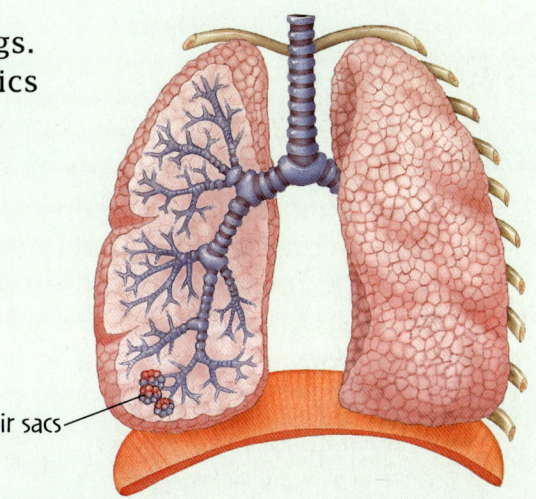

air sacs

poison

A poison is a chemical which badly affects or kills a living thing.

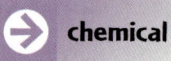
→ chemical

Snakes inject their poison through hollow teeth.

pole (magnetic)

The end of a magnet is called the pole. It can either be a north or south pole. A north pole attracts another south pole (unlike poles attract). Two south poles repel each other (like poles repel).

The north pole of a magnet points to the North Pole of the Earth.

pollen

Pollen is a very fine powder. It is released by the anthers of a flower. Pollen fertilizes the female ovules to make a seed.

→ allergy, anther, fertilize, male, ovule, pollinate

pollen

pollinate

Pollination happens when pollen comes into contact with the female parts of a flower.

In the mountains of South America hummingbirds are the main pollinators.

→ flower, grass, pollen

pollution

Pollution is anything that spoils the environment. Untreated sewage pollutes rivers.

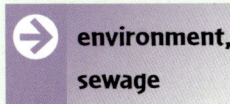 environment, sewage

Smoke pollutes the air.

powder

Powder is a mass of dry dust or very small particles.

Flour and icing sugar are powders, but granulated sugar is too gritty to be called a powder.

precipitation

Precipitation is water that falls to the ground as rain, hail, sleet, or snow.

Precipitation occurs when the droplets in clouds become heavy and fall.

 water cycle

predator

Animals that catch and eat other animals are predators.

 carnivore, prey

Sharks are ocean predators.

pressure

Pressure is a force pressing on an area. A force pressing on a small area produces more pressure than the same force spread over a large area.

Snowshoes spread your weight over a larger area so that there is less pressure on the snow.

prey

Animals that are hunted and eaten by predators are called prey.

barn owl (predator)

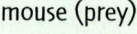

mouse (prey)

 **carnivore, food chain, predator**

prism

A prism is a shaped piece of glass. It can split white light into the colours of the spectrum.

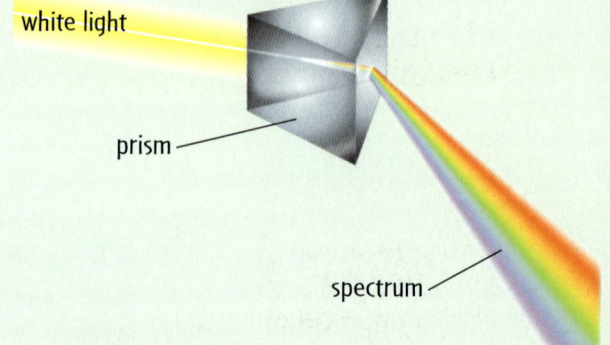

white light

prism

spectrum

 colour, light, spectrum

producer

All green plants make food in their leaves from air, water, and light. They are the only producers of food.

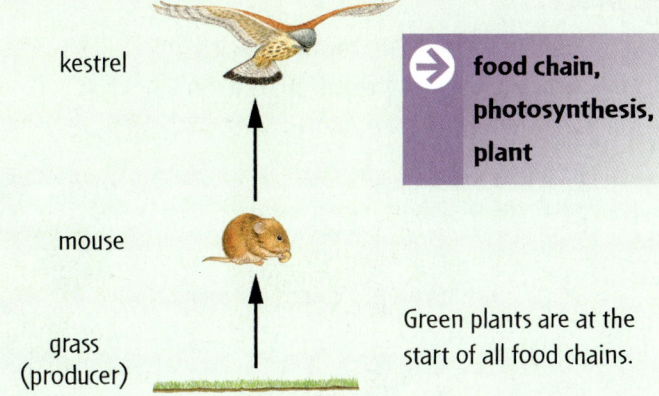

kestrel

mouse

grass
(producer)

food chain, photosynthesis, plant

Green plants are at the start of all food chains.

protein

People need to eat some protein as part of their diet. Protein helps build the body's tissues.

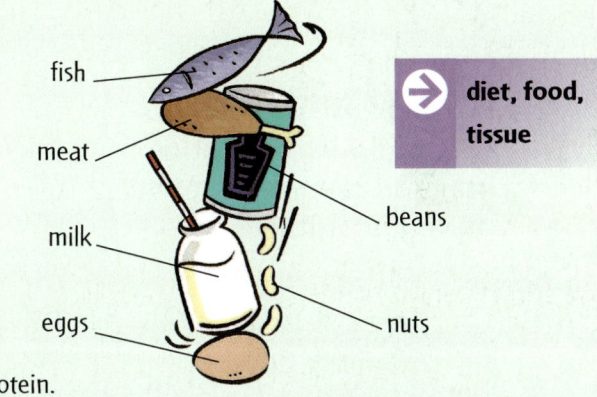

fish

meat

milk

eggs

beans

nuts

diet, food, tissue

These foods are good sources of protein.

puberty

Puberty is the time when children begin to change into adults. Girls begin to menstruate and their genitals get larger. Boys grow face hair, their voices get lower, and their genitals get larger.

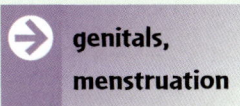
genitals, menstruation

Both boys and girls grow quickly but boys eventually grow bigger than girls.

pulse

Each time the heart beats it can be felt as a pulse in the arteries.

after running: 140 beats per minute

resting pulse: 75 beats per minute

 artery, blood, heart

pupa (plural pupae)

The pupa is the resting stage of an insect between larva and adult.

 caterpillar, chrysalis, insect, larva

pupa

adult (peacock butterfly)

larva (caterpillar)

The pupa of a butterfly is called a chrysalis.

pupil

The hole in the centre of your eye is the pupil. Light goes into the eye through the pupil.

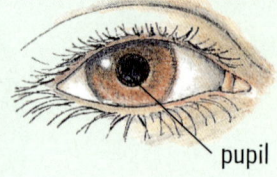

pupil

 eye, iris, light

Qq

quartz

Rock crystal or quartz is a very common mineral. A lot of sand is made from quartz grains.

mineral

Quartz sometimes forms large crystals.

Rr

radiation

Radiation is energy that can travel through space at the speed of light. Light, heat, X-rays, and radio waves are all forms of radiation.

cancer, light, heat, X-ray

radioactive

In some types of atom, the nucleus gives off particles and energy in the form of radioactivity.

Radioactive materials are dangerous. Some of them can cause fatal illness.

radioactive warning sign

nucleus

rainbow

A rainbow is formed when sunlight passes through drops of rain. The raindrops act like tiny prisms.

colour, light, prism

Rainbows always appear opposite the Sun.

react

When chemicals react they combine together, or split apart, or join up in new ways. This makes new chemicals.

Cooking almost always involves chemical reactions.

 chemical, irreversible change, rust

reflect

We see objects because they reflect light. When shiny surfaces reflect light the light makes an image.

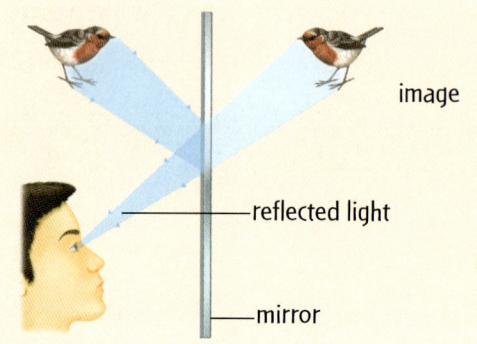

image

reflected light

mirror

 image, mirror

Shiny surfaces reflect more of the light than dull surfaces.

refract

When light is refracted it is bent as it passes from one transparent material to another.

 light, transparent

Light is refracted as it passes from air to glass, and from glass to air.

reproduction (asexual)

All types of living things can make copies of themselves. This is called reproduction. There is sexual and asexual reproduction.

Asexual reproduction does not involve male and female cells. Only one parent is needed. Asexual reproduction occurs mostly in plants and bacteria. It is rare in animals except in a few simple kinds like the worm.

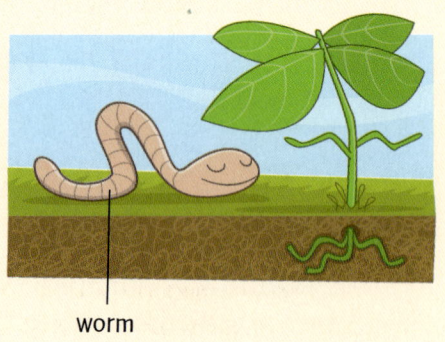

worm

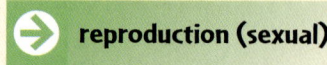 **reproduction (sexual)**

reproduction (sexual)

All types of living things can make copies of themselves. This is called reproduction. There is sexual and asexual reproduction.

parents   young

1. When animals reproduce sexually, a sperm cell from a male animal combines with an egg from a female to produce a baby.

2. When plants reproduce sexually, the male and female parts of the plant are involved.

anthers (male)   stigma (female)

➜ **reproduction (asexual), sexual intercourse**

reptile

Reptiles are cold-blooded animals with dry, scaly skin. They lay leathery eggs.

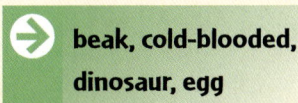

➜ **beak, cold-blooded, dinosaur, egg**

python

crocodile   chameleon

All these are reptiles.

resistance (electricity)

All conductors slow the flow of electricity. This is called resistance.

Very thin conductors like the filament of this bulb have more resistance than thick pieces of the same material.

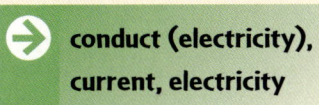

➜ **conduct (electricity), current, electricity**

filament

respiration

Respiration is the process in which sugar is broken down in the body to give energy. In animals oxygen is needed to do this and carbon dioxide is excreted. Both animals and plants respire.

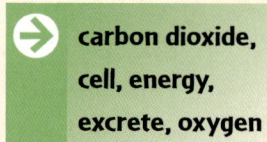 **carbon dioxide, cell, energy, excrete, oxygen**

When we exercise we use a lot of energy and need to breathe in more oxygen.

retina

The retina is the part of the eye on which light falls after it has passed through the pupil. It is a mass of nerve endings which react to light.

eye, nerve, pupil

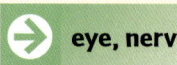
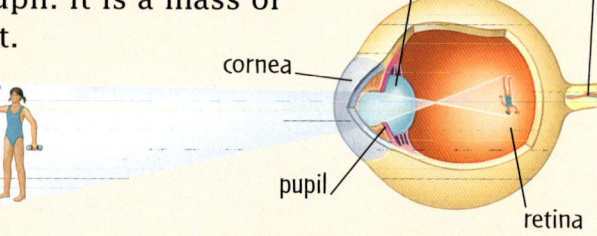

lens   optic nerve

cornea

pupil

retina

reversible change

Changes that can be switched back are reversible.

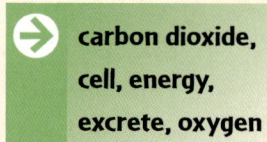 **dissolve, freeze, irreversible change, melt, state of matter**

Sugar dissolves in water. But put the solution in the sun for a few days and the water will evaporate, leaving sugar again.

rock

Rocks are mixtures of minerals. There are three different types of rock: igneous, metamorphic, and sedimentary.

 fossil, igneous rock, metamorphic rock, mineral, sedimentary rock

This rock has fossil leaves on it.

rocket

A rocket is a device that shoots gases out behind it to thrust the machine forward.

root

The part of a plant that anchors it in the soil is called the root. Roots take in water for the plant. Some store water as well.

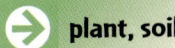 plant, soil

We eat many types of root, such as carrots and turnips.

rot

When a plant or animal dies its body begins to fall apart. This process is known as rotting.

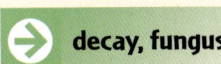 decay, fungus

Living things such as fungi depend upon rotten material for food.

rotate

When an object rotates it turns on its axis. The Earth turns on its axis once each day.

 axis, day, Earth

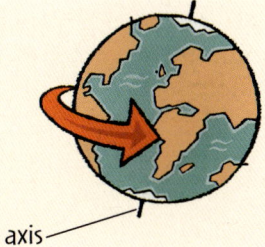

axis

rust

Rust is iron oxide. It forms when iron reacts with water and oxygen from the air.

 iron, oxide, react

Iron tools left out in the rain will go rusty.

Ss

salt

The salt we put on our food is a chemical made from sodium and chlorine. It is called sodium chloride.

Salt is mined from rocks or distilled from seawater. It forms cube-shaped crystals.

 chemical, crystal, distil

satellite

An object that orbits a planet is called a satellite. Moons are natural satellites. People have made artificial satellites to help with communications on Earth.

Hundreds of artificial satellites orbit the Earth.

 Moon, orbit, planet

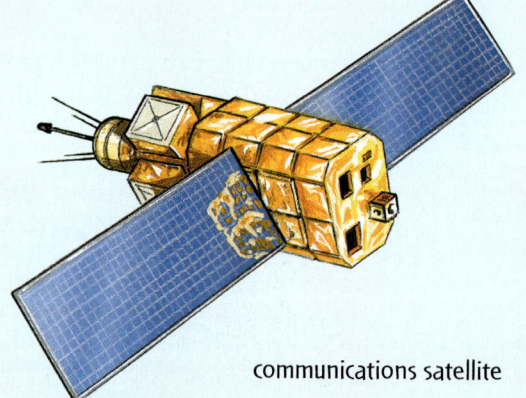

communications satellite

saturated

A solution is saturated when no more solid can be dissolved in it.

dissolve, solute, solution, solvent

scale

Scales are overlapping plates that cover an animal's body. On fish they are tough, but on butterfly's wings they are very delicate.

 fish, reptile

Fish scales are made of keratin, which is the same material that our fingernails are made from.

season

Seasons are periods of similar weather. In places like Europe there are four seasons, but many tropical areas have two, the wet and the dry season.

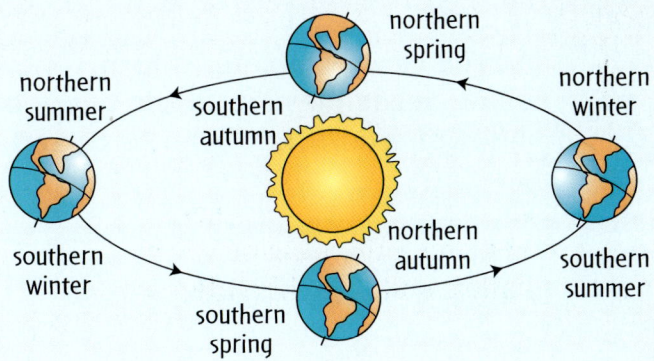

When it is summer in the northern hemisphere it is winter in the south.

sediment

Sediment is a solid that settles at the bottom of a liquid.

After a storm the sediment in a river is stirred up, and the river becomes cloudy and muddy.

sedimentary rock

Sedimentary rock is formed when sediment collects at the bottom of a lake or sea.

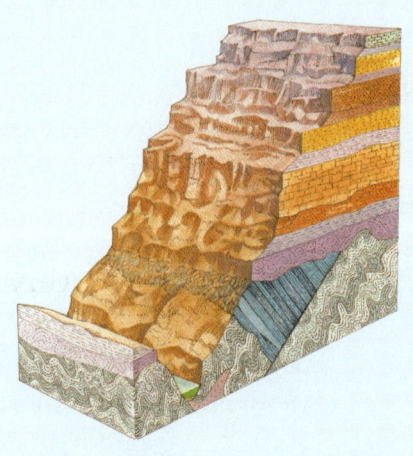

The walls of the Grand Canyon are made of layers of sedimentary rocks.

 rock

seed

A seed can germinate to form a new plant. Seeds develop in the ovary of a flower after it has been fertilized.

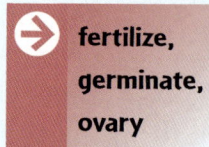

→ fertilize, germinate, ovary

A seed contains food for the developing plant.

seedling

A young plant is called a seedling.

semen

The fluid that contains the male sperm is called semen. It is passed to the female during sexual intercourse.

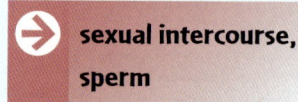

→ sexual intercourse, sperm

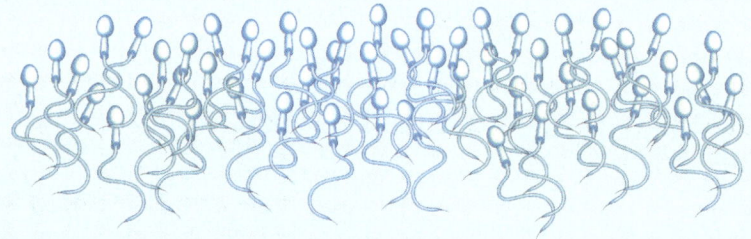

Each teaspoon of semen contains millions of sperms.

senses

Humans have five senses: sight, smell, touch, taste, hearing.

eyes (sight)
ears (hearing)
nose (smell)
tongue (taste)
fingers (touch)

Animals and people use their senses to detect what is happening around them.

sepal

Before a flower opens it is protected by sepals.

sepal

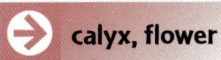
calyx, flower

series circuit

An electrical circuit that has only one path through it is called a series circuit.

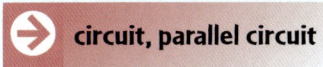
circuit, parallel circuit

sewage

Waste water from lavatories and drains is called sewage. It is treated with useful bacteria to break it down and make it harmless.

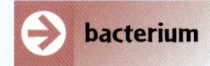
bacterium

Waste water is treated at a sewage works.

sexual intercourse

In sexual intercourse the male inserts his penis into the female's vagina. His sperm can fertilize the female's egg to make a baby.

→ **fertilize, genitals, penis, reproduction (asexual), reproduction (sexual), sperm, vagina**

silicon

Silicon is an element. It is used to make silicon chips.

→ **element**

Silicon chips are used in things like computers, calculators, and CD players.

skeleton

Vertebrates have an internal skeleton made of bone. Insects and many other invertebrates have an external skeleton.

→ **bone, invertebrate, vertebrate**

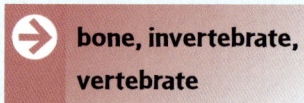

frog
(internal skeleton or endoskeleton)

scorpion
(external skeleton or exoskeleton)

skin

The covering of animals is called skin. Mammals have hairy skin. Reptiles and fish have scaly skin. Birds' skin is covered in feathers. The skin of amphibians is smooth and damp.

A polar bear has black skin! You can see this around its nose.

 amphibian, bird, cell, fish, mammal, reptile

skull

The skull is the name for the bones of the head. This includes the jaw.

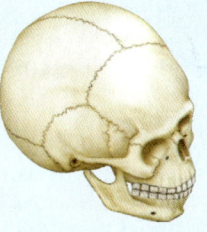

 cranium

snow

Snow is water frozen into single ice crystals. These crystals clump together to form snowflakes.

crystal, freeze, state of matter

Snowflakes have six arms.

soil

Soil is ground up rock mixed with plant and animal remains.

topsoil rich in humus

subsoil with little humus

 humus, rock

bedrock

solar power

Solar power is the use of energy from the Sun. Some people put solar panels on their houses to trap solar energy which is used to heat water in the house.

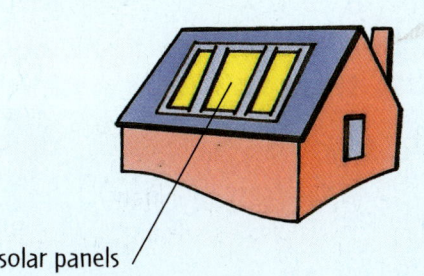

solar panels

Solar System

The Solar System is the Sun and its orbiting planets.

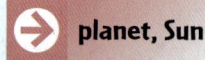 planet, Sun

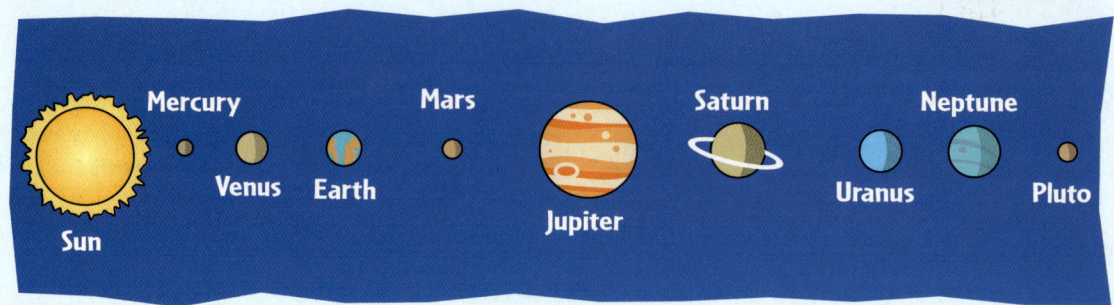

solid

Materials that hold their shape and can be cut are solid.

 gas, liquid

Rocks can be cut, but it's hard work!

solstice

See midsummer and midwinter.

soluble

Solids and gases that dissolve in a liquid are soluble.

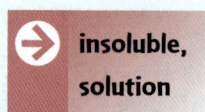 insoluble, solution

Sugar is soluble in water.

solute

A solute is a solid or gas that will dissolve in a liquid.

 solution

In this solution carbon dioxide is the solute.

solution

A solution is a mixture of a liquid with a dissolved solid or gas.

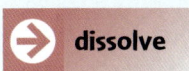 dissolve

Coffee is a solution.

solvent

A solvent is a liquid that will dissolve a solid or a gas.

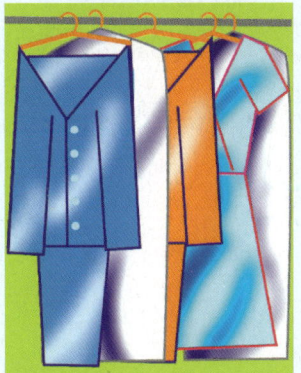

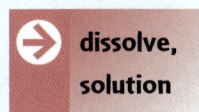 dissolve, solution

Water is not used in dry cleaning. Other solvents are used to dissolve grease and dirt.

sound

Vibrations cause sound. We hear sound with our ears.

When you hit a drum, the drumskin vibrates and makes a sound.

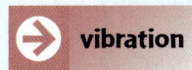 vibration

space

Space is everything outside the Earth's atmosphere. Most of space is a vacuum.

Space probes have left our Solar System and are exploring space between the stars.

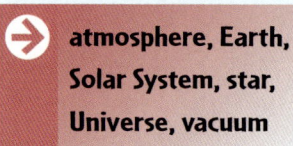

→ **atmosphere, Earth, Solar System, star, Universe, vacuum**

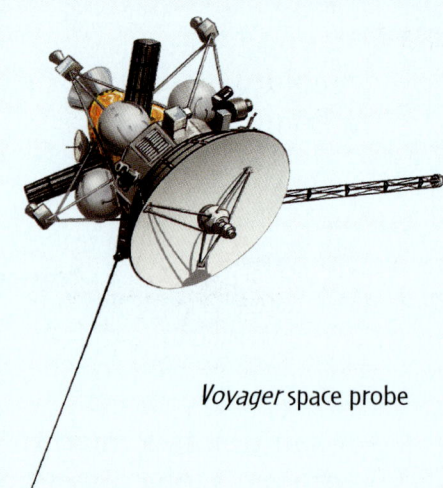

Voyager space probe

species

Types of living things are called species. We are the human species. Scientists call our species *Homo sapiens*.

cheetah

tiger

Tigers and cheetahs are two different species from the cat family.

spectrum (plural spectra)

The spectrum is all the colours of the rainbow.

 colour, light, prism, rainbow

sperm

Sperm are single cells produced by male animals. Sperm fertilize the female's eggs.

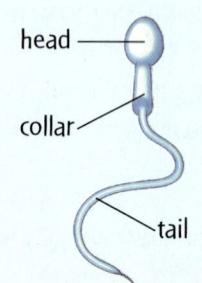

head
collar
tail

A sperm cell swims using its tail. Sperm cells are tiny compared with the female egg.

 fertilize, male, pollen, semen

spine

The backbone of vertebrate animals is also called the spine.

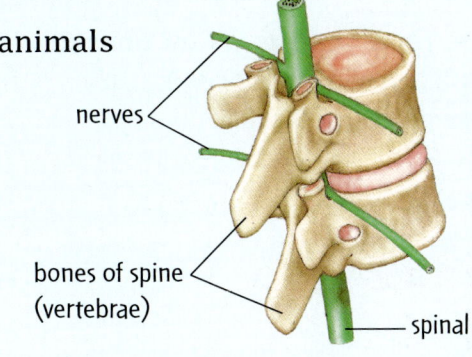

The nerves of the spinal cord run in a tube up the spine.

nerves

bones of spine (vertebrae)

spinal cord

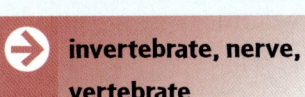

→ invertebrate, nerve, vertebrate

spore

Spores are like seeds but they are much smaller. Spores are used for reproduction by fungi, bacteria, ferns, and mosses.

The spores produced by fungi make lovely patterns on paper.

→ bacterium, fungus, seed

stamen

The male parts of a flower are called the stamen.

The anther and filament together make up the stamen.

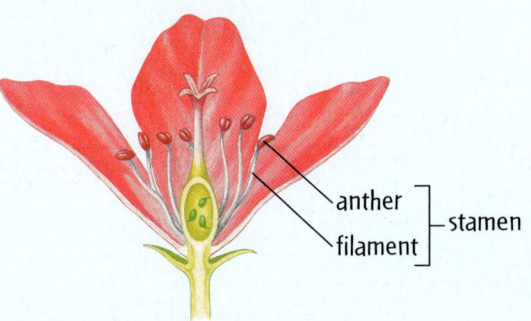

anther

filament

stamen

→ anther, flower, male, pollen

star

A star is a huge ball of glowing hydrogen gas. The Sun is our closest star.

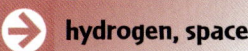

→ hydrogen, space

The stars in the night sky are so far away that they look like points of light.

starch

Starch is food that gives us energy. Bread, pasta, maize, cereals, and potatoes contain starch.

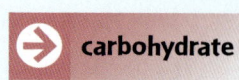

carbohydrate

These foods are full of starch.

state of matter

Matter can be in three states: solid, liquid, or gas. This can also be called a "phase of matter".

gas, liquid, solid

The ice cubes and the kitchen units are solid. The water and oil are liquid. The flame is burning gas.

steel

Steel is made from iron. Small amounts of other metals or carbon are added to the iron.

 carbon, iron, rust

Many tools are made from hardened steel.

sterile

Anything that is totally without life is sterile.

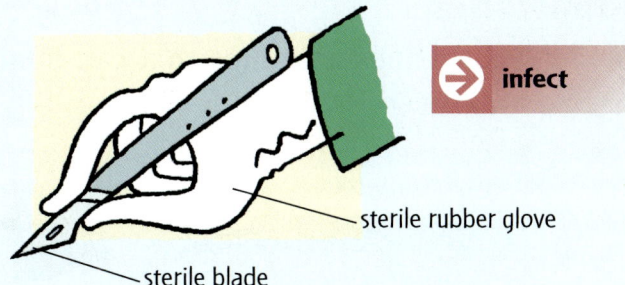

infect

This blade must be sterile to avoid infection during an operation.

sterile rubber glove

sterile blade

stethoscope

A doctor uses a stethoscope to listen to the chest or stomach of a patient.

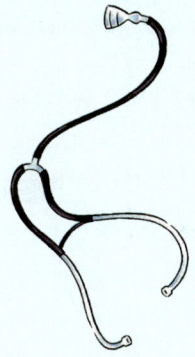

Sound travels up the two hollow tubes to the doctor's ears.

stigma

The stigma is the top of the female part of the flower. It is sticky so pollen grains get caught on its surface.

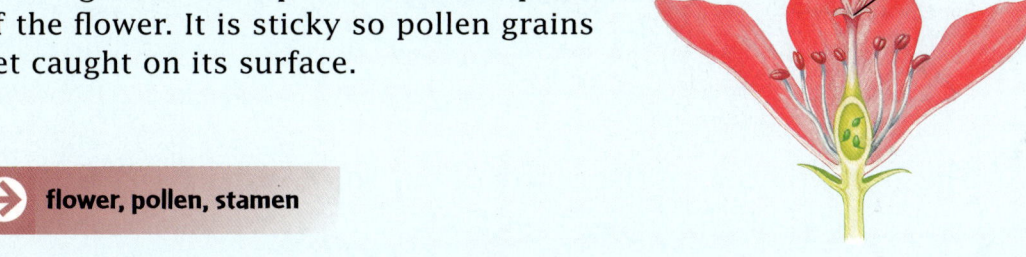

stigma

flower, pollen, stamen

stomach

The stomach is a bag in which the digestion of food begins.

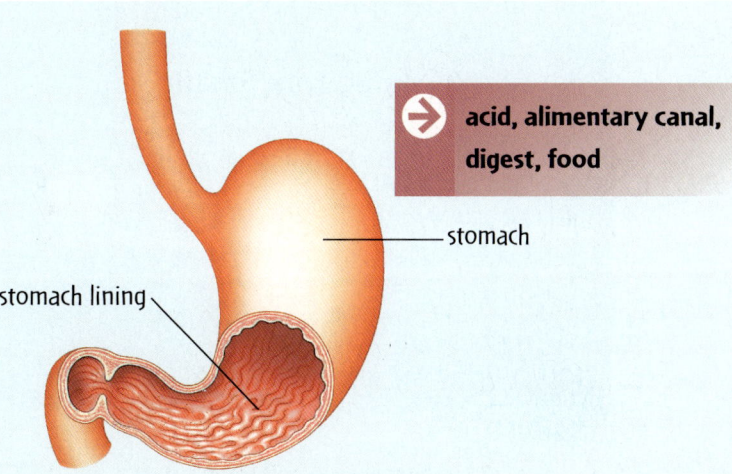

acid, alimentary canal, digest, food

stomach

stomach lining

There is very strong acid in the stomach.

submarine

Submarines are ships that can float below the surface of the water.

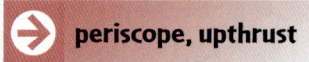 periscope, upthrust

floating · · · diving · · · surfacing

sugar

Sugar is a sweet food that gives energy. There are several types of sugar.

→ carbohydrate

Sugar is the main ingredient in sweets.

Sun

The Sun is the star at the centre of our Solar System.

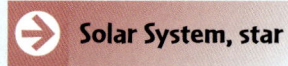 Solar System, star

The temperature at the Sun's surface is 6 000 °C, but at the core it is 15 million °C.

sundial

A sundial uses the position of a shadow to tell the time. The shadow's position changes as the Sun moves across the sky.

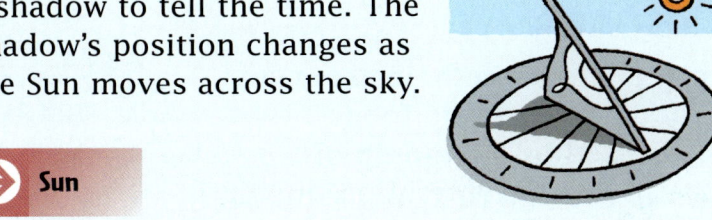

➔ Sun

sweat

Sweat is salty water which oozes out of our skin. As it evaporates it cools our body.

➔ evaporate

switch

A switch is part of an electrical circuit that can stop or allow electricity to flow.

If this switch is tilted it will complete a circuit and turn the light on.

➔ electric symbols

synthetic

Materials that are synthetic have been manufactured. Nylon and glass are both synthetic materials.

➔ manufactured, natural

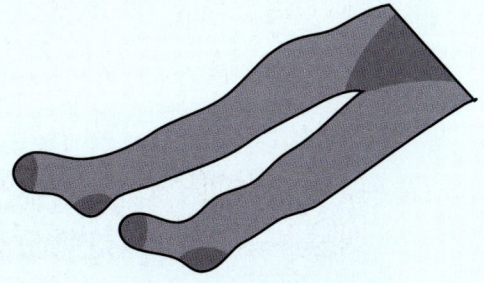

These tights are made of nylon.

Tt

teeth

There are three main kinds of teeth. Incisors cut food. Canines rip food. Molars grind food. Tooth decay can be caused by a build-up of sticky plaque on teeth. This feeds acid-producing bacteria. This acid eats away at the teeth.

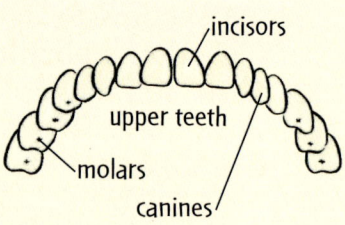

incisors

upper teeth

molars

canines

lower teeth

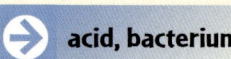 **acid, bacterium**

Humans have a mixture of teeth, because we eat a variety of foods.

telescope

A telescope is a tube with lenses or mirrors which magnify a distant object.

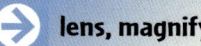 **lens, magnify**

temperature

An object's temperature is a measure of how hot it is. Temperature is measured in degrees Celsius (°C).

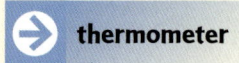 **thermometer**

Iron melts at a temperature of over 1500°C.

testicle

Sperm are produced in the testicles.

 **sperm**

Testicles are held away from the rest of the body to keep them cool.

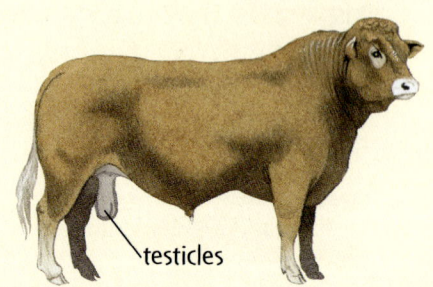

testicles

thermometer

A thermometer is a device for measuring temperature.

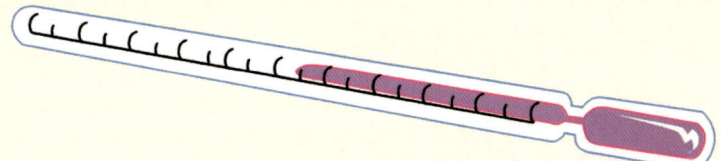

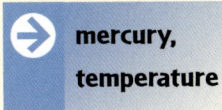
→ mercury, temperature

Clinical thermometers are used to take people's temperature.

thorax

The thorax is another word for the chest.

→ insect

An insect's thorax is the middle part of its body. Its legs and wings are attached to the thorax.

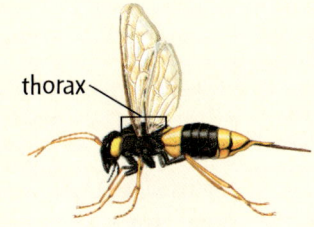
thorax

thunder

Thunder is the noise made when lightning flashes from clouds. We hear the sound after we see the light because sound travels much more slowly than light.

→ lightning, sound

tide

The tide is the daily rise and fall of the level of the sea. In many places there are two high tides and two low tides each day. Tides are caused by the gravity of the Moon pulling on the oceans.

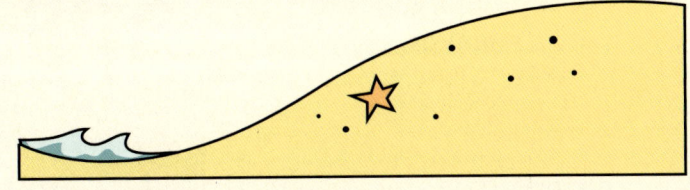

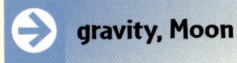
→ gravity, Moon

In some places the tide only rises and falls once a day.

tissue

The bodies of living things are made from tissue of many different types. Muscle tissue, skin tissue, and nerve tissue are examples of tissue types.

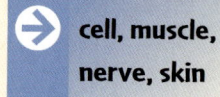 cell, muscle, nerve, skin

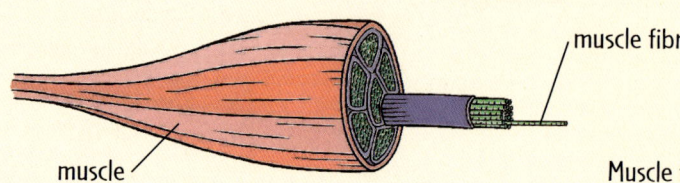

muscle fibre

muscle

Muscle tissue is made up of bundles of tiny fibres.

translucent

Translucent materials let through some light, but they are not completely see-through.

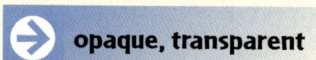 opaque, transparent

transparent

Transparent materials are completely see-through. Clear glass and clear plastic are both transparent.

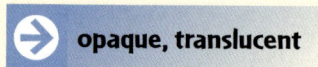 opaque, translucent

transpiration

In transpiration, water drawn up by the roots of a plant evaporates off its leaves.

 evaporate

As water is lost from the leaves more water is drawn up through the roots.

Uu

ultrasound

Ultrasound is sound that is at a pitch above that which humans can hear.

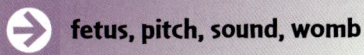
fetus, pitch, sound, womb

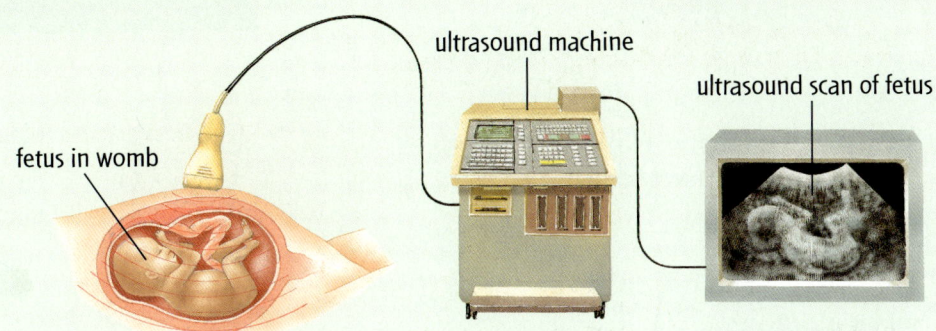

fetus in womb

ultrasound machine

ultrasound scan of fetus

Ultrasound easily passes through skin and muscle. Doctors use it to check on the development of a fetus in the womb.

ultraviolet

Ultraviolet is an invisible kind of radiation similar to light. Ultraviolet rays from the Sun turn white people's skin brown.

ozone

Too much ultraviolet can burn the skin.

umbilical cord

All the time the fetus is inside its mother she feeds it through the umbilical cord. Your belly button is left in the place where the cord entered your body.

fetus

umbilical cord

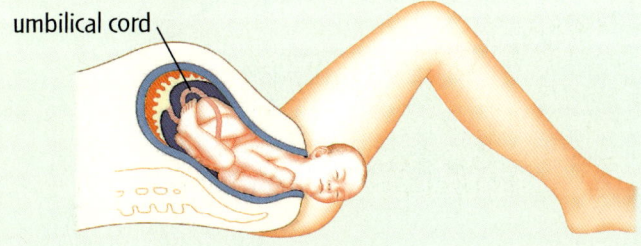

The umbilical cord carries blood containing oxygen and food to the baby.

Universe

There are billions of stars in each galaxy and billions of galaxies in the Universe. The Universe is everything there is. It is everything we can see or imagine.

upthrust

Upthrust is the force that makes objects float in water or in air.

Upthrust is greater than the force of gravity on this balloon so it rises.

 force

urine

Urine is a mixture of waste chemicals from the body dissolved in water. Urine is excreted by the kidneys and stored in the bladder before it passes out of the body.

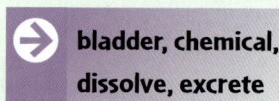 bladder, chemical, dissolve, excrete

The chemicals in urine make it a good fertilizer.

uterus

A baby develops inside its mother's uterus.

Another name for the uterus is the womb.

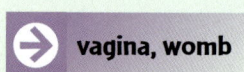 vagina, womb

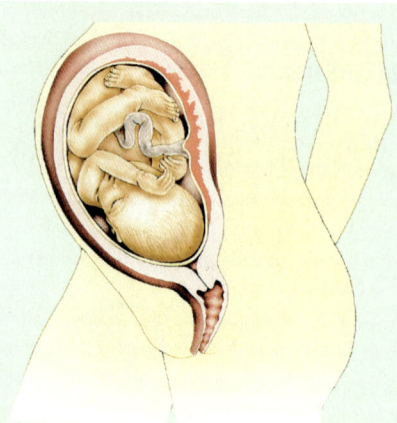

Vv

vaccinate

See immunize.

vacuum

A vacuum is a space that is completely empty. There is no air in a vacuum.

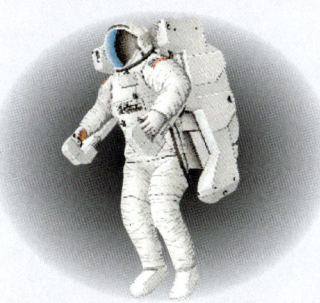

 space

There is no air in space so astronauts need to carry air tanks.

vagina

The vagina is the female sexual opening. It leads to the womb (uterus).

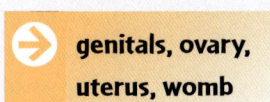 genitals, ovary, uterus, womb

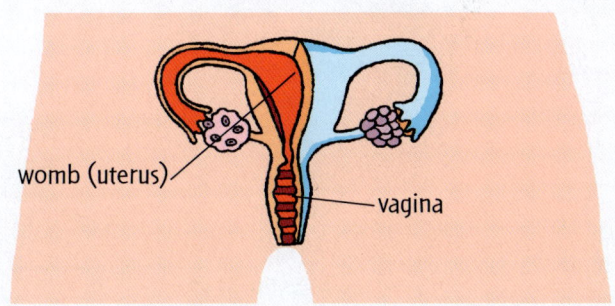

womb (uterus)

vagina

vapour

A vapour is a gas. Water vapour is the gas form of water.

 condense, evaporate, state of matter

Water vapour from the clothes makes the air feel damp.

vegetation

The plants that grow in a place are called vegetation.

Trees, grass, and flowering plants are the vegetation in this field.

 plant

vein

In many animals blood is carried back to the heart in veins.

You can easily see the veins on the back of an old person's hand.

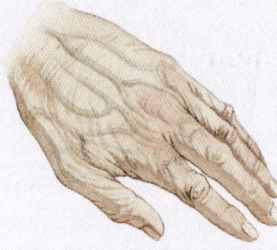

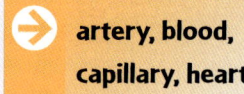
artery, blood, capillary, heart

vertebrate

Vertebrates are animals that have a backbone.

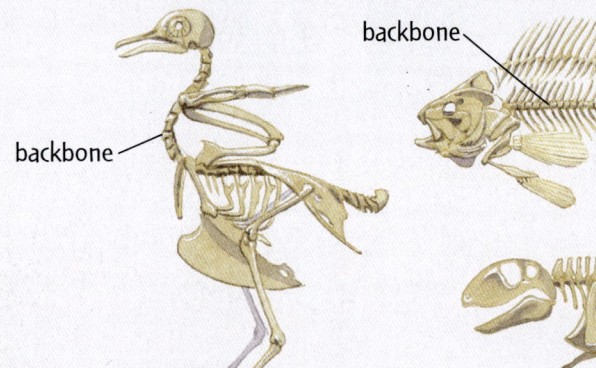
backbone

backbone

backbone

amphibian, bird, fish, mammal, reptile

vibration

An object that moves backwards and forwards is vibrating. Vibrations cause sounds.

sound

The vibrations of the cymbals make the air vibrate.

virus

Viruses are tiny micro-organisms. They are much smaller than bacteria. They can only live in the cells of other living things.

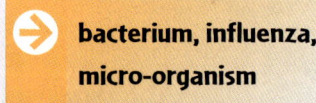
bacterium, influenza, micro-organism

Colds and 'flu are caused by viruses.

vitamin

Vitamins are chemicals in food which keep us healthy.

chemical, food

Oranges and lemons contain lots of vitamin C.

volcano

A volcano is a mountain that has been built up from flows of lava or ash. A volcano that no longer erupts is called extinct.

 lava, magma, rock

volt

Volts are a measure of the energy of a flow of electricity. Mains electricity carries a voltage of 210–240 volts.

 electricity, energy

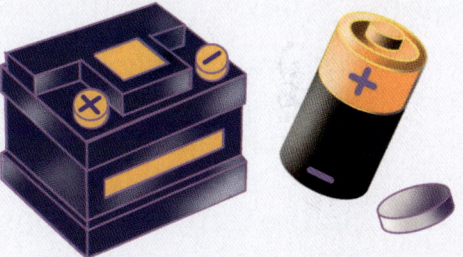

Batteries are low voltage (1.5–12 volts) compared with mains electricity.

volume

Volume is the space taken up by an object.

 density

You can find out what the volume of a liquid is by using a measuring jug.

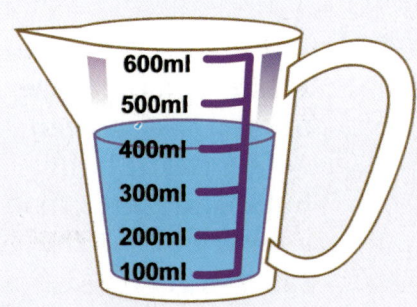

600ml
500ml
400ml
300ml
200ml
100ml

warm-blooded

Animals that keep their temperature at a constant level are called warm-blooded. Birds and mammals can do this because they have coverings of feathers, fur, or fat. This keeps their heat in.

The feathers and fat of a penguin keep it warm even in the Antarctic .

 bird, cold-blooded, fat, feather, mammal

water

Pure water is transparent, colourless, and does not smell. We need about 2 litres of water a day to keep us healthy.

below 0°C

between 0°C and 100°C

above 100°C

solid

liquid

gas

 gas, liquid, solid, vapour

water cycle

The water cycle is the never-ending process of water moving from the oceans, up into the atmosphere, and back to the Earth and oceans.

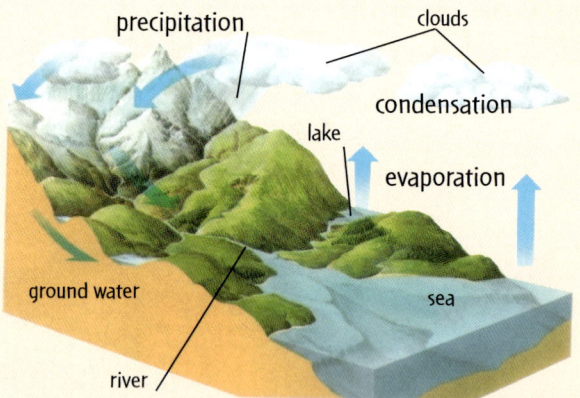

precipitation

clouds

condensation

lake

evaporation

ground water

sea

river

 condense, evaporate

watt

A watt is a measure of electrical power. A 100-W (watt) light bulb is brighter than a 60-W bulb of the same type.

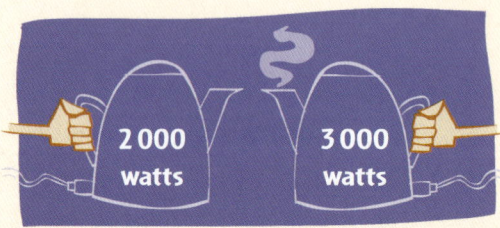

2 000 watts

3 000 watts

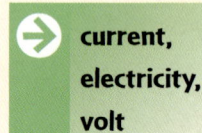 **current, electricity, volt**

The 3 000-W kettle boils more quickly than a 2 000-W one.

weather

Weather is the rain, wind, sunshine, snow, or other conditions that you get at a particular time and place.

 climate, precipitation

weight

Weight is the pull of gravity on a mass. In science, weight is measured in newtons.

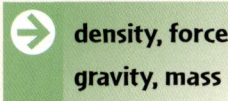 density, force, gravity, mass

The cabbage has a mass of 300 grams. Its weight is three newtons.

womb

The womb is the organ in females where the baby grows.

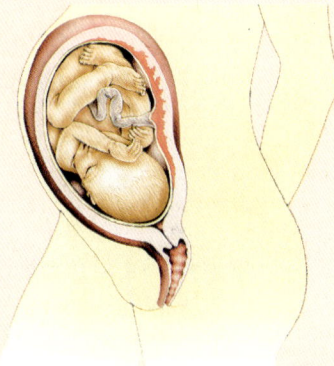

Another name for womb is uterus.

 female, organ, uterus

work

Work is the ability to make things move or get hot.

 energy

When a crane lifts up a load, it is doing work.

X-ray

X-rays are a form of energy that can pass through most materials. They can pass more easily through muscle than through bone.

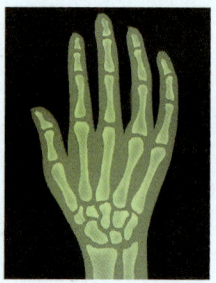

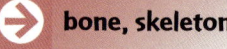
bone, skeleton

year

The Earth takes one year to orbit the Sun. A year is 365 $\frac{1}{4}$ days.

Earth, orbit, Sun

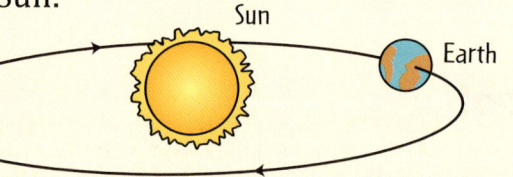
Sun
Earth

yeast

Yeast is a type of fungus. It is a micro-organism that is used in bread and beer making.

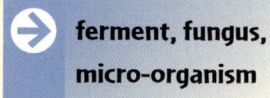
ferment, fungus, micro-organism

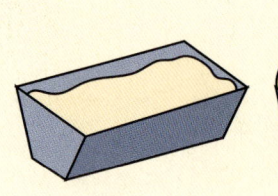  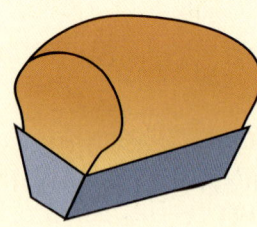

The carbon dioxide released by yeast makes bread rise.

yolk

The yolk is the yellow part of an egg. It is the food supply for the growing chick.

bird, reptile

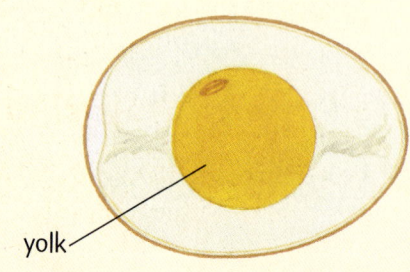
yolk

Zz

zinc

Zinc is a soft silvery-grey metal. It does not rust so it is used to coat steel buckets, lamp posts, and crash barriers.

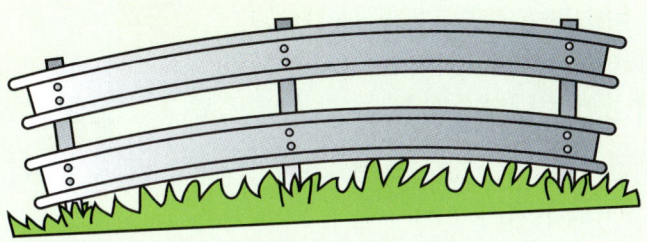
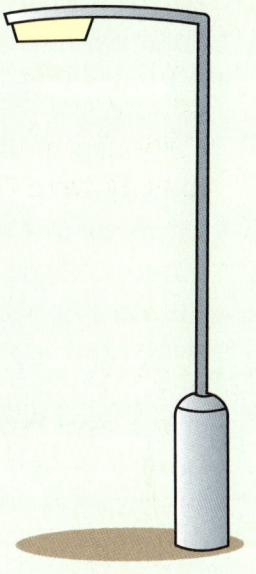

When iron is coated in zinc it is said to be galvanized.

zoology

Zoology is the study of animals.

Apparatus

force meter

Spring balances are a type of force meter. We use them to measure the pull of gravity. Force is measured in newtons.

balance

Balances are used to measure the mass of objects. Gram and kilogram masses are put on one side. The object being measured is put on the other side.

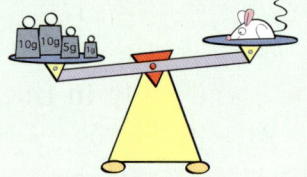

ruler and callipers

Length is measured in metres and centimetres. Callipers can measure the diameter of a ball.

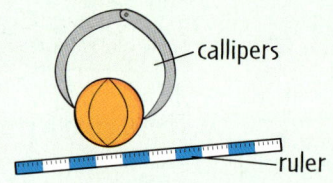

voltmeter and ammeter

Voltmeters measure the voltage change between different parts of a circuit. Ammeters measure the flow of electricity round a circuit.

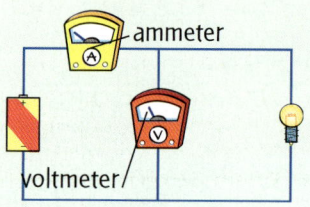

thermometer

Temperature is measured using thermometers. Each type of thermometer measures a different range of temperatures. Clinical thermometers only measure temperatures which are close to normal body temperature.

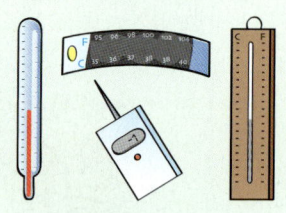

microscope

Microscopes show magnified images of tiny objects.

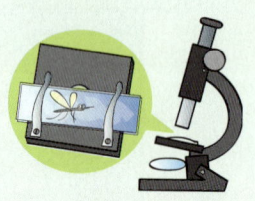

telescope

Telescopes magnify distant objects. The Hubble space telescope gives a view of very distant objects.

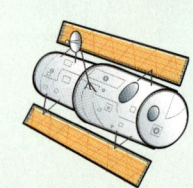

The Human Body

The human body is made up of a number of different systems. Each system does a special job.

- The skeleton holds up the rest of the body and protects organs such as the heart and brain.
- Muscles pull on the skeleton enabling us to move.
- The circulation of blood takes food and oxygen to the body's cells, and takes away waste products.
- The kidneys clean waste from the blood, which passes out of the body in the urine.
- The nervous system senses the environment and passes messages and commands around the body.
- The digestive system takes in food and breaks it down ready for use by the body.

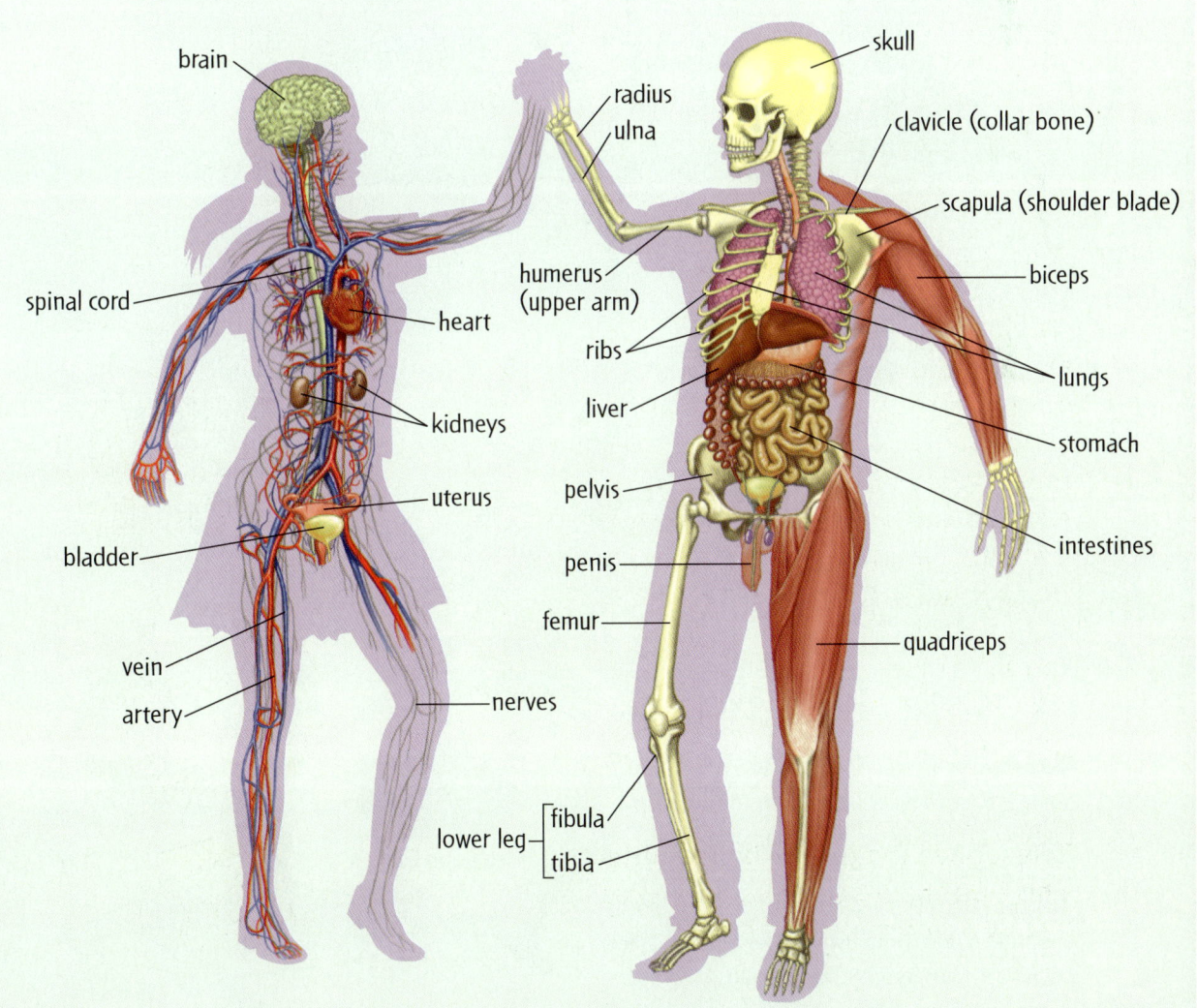

brain

radius

ulna

skull

clavicle (collar bone)

scapula (shoulder blade)

spinal cord

heart

humerus (upper arm)

biceps

ribs

kidneys

liver

lungs

stomach

uterus

pelvis

intestines

bladder

penis

vein

femur

quadriceps

artery

nerves

lower leg — fibula, tibia

Classification of Animals

Unlike plants, animals cannot make their own food. They have to eat other living things to survive. The animal kingdom can be divided into vertebrates and invertebrates. Vertebrates are animals that have backbones, such as fish, reptiles, and mammals. Invertebrates are animals that do not have backbones.

Vertebrates are all more closely related to each other than to other animals, so they are a proper scientific grouping. However, invertebrates are not a proper scientific grouping because the different types of invertebrate are not closely related to each other.

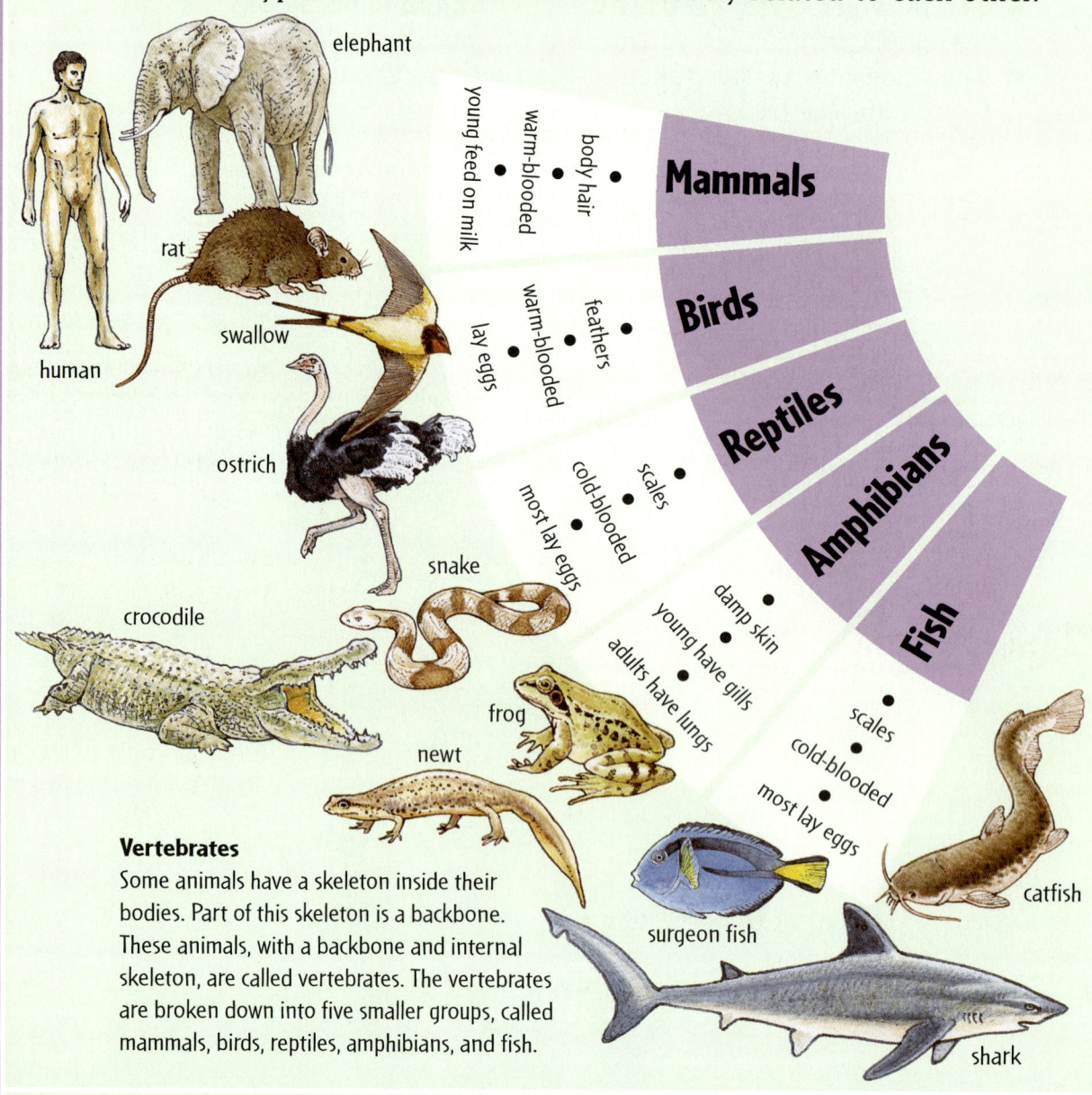

elephant

rat

swallow

human

ostrich

snake

crocodile

frog

newt

surgeon fish

catfish

shark

young feed on milk
warm-blooded
body hair
Mammals

lay eggs
warm-blooded
feathers
Birds

most lay eggs
cold-blooded
scales
Reptiles

damp skin
young have gills
adults have lungs
Amphibians

scales
cold-blooded
most lay eggs
Fish

Vertebrates

Some animals have a skeleton inside their bodies. Part of this skeleton is a backbone. These animals, with a backbone and internal skeleton, are called vertebrates. The vertebrates are broken down into five smaller groups, called mammals, birds, reptiles, amphibians, and fish.

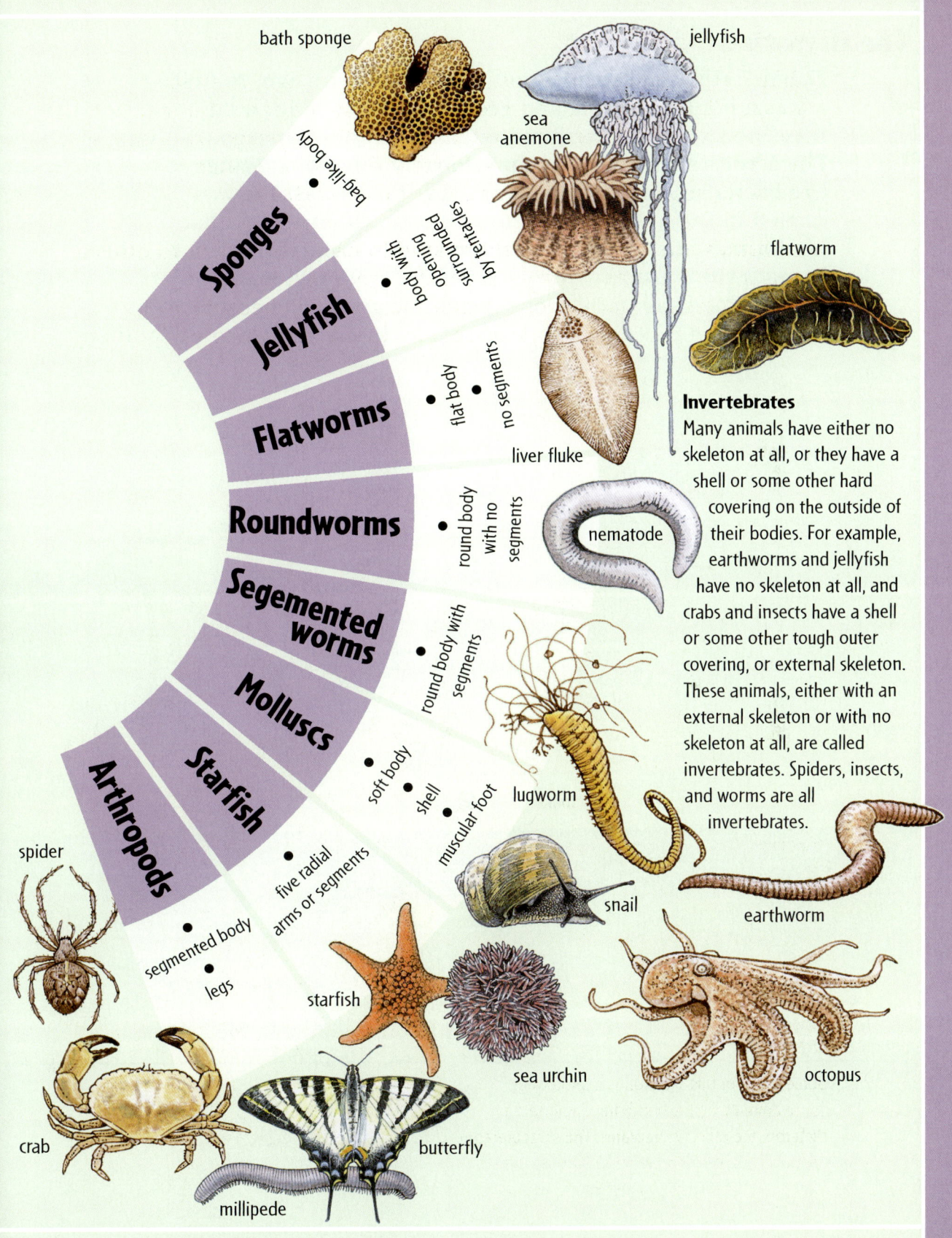

bath sponge

jellyfish

sea anemone

flatworm

Sponges

bag-like body

Jellyfish

body with opening surrounded by tentacles

Flatworms

flat body

no segments

liver fluke

Invertebrates

Many animals have either no skeleton at all, or they have a shell or some other hard covering on the outside of their bodies. For example, earthworms and jellyfish have no skeleton at all, and crabs and insects have a shell or some other tough outer covering, or external skeleton. These animals, either with an external skeleton or with no skeleton at all, are called invertebrates. Spiders, insects, and worms are all invertebrates.

Roundworms

round body with no segments

nematode

Segemented worms

round body with segments

lugworm

earthworm

Molluscs

soft body

shell

muscular foot

snail

Starfish

five radial arms or segments

starfish

sea urchin

octopus

Arthropods

spider

segmented body

legs

crab

butterfly

millipede

151

The History of Life

Planet Earth was formed about 4½ billion years ago. At first it was a hot ball of rock and gas on which nothing could live. Life started on Earth more than 3 billion years ago. The earliest forms of life were probably tiny living things like bacteria. Some scientists say that the earliest life was carried to Earth on a meteorite or comet. Others think that life formed from chemicals on the Earth's surface or deep beneath the ocean.

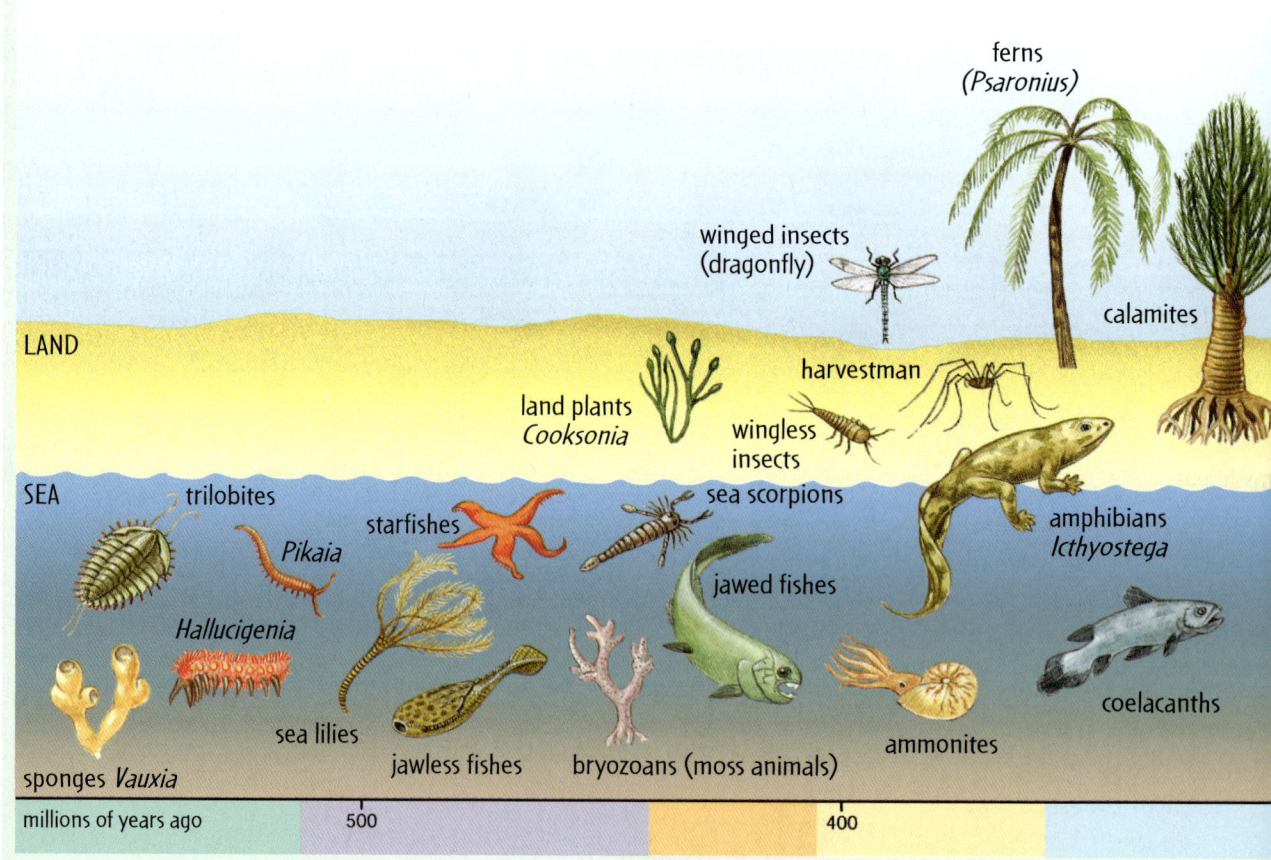

ferns
(*Psaronius*)

winged insects
(dragonfly)

calamites

LAND

harvestman

land plants
Cooksonia

wingless
insects

SEA   trilobites

sea scorpions

amphibians
Icthyostega

starfishes

Pikaia

jawed fishes

Hallucigenia

coelacanths

sea lilies

jawless fishes   bryozoans (moss animals)   ammonites

sponges *Vauxia*

millions of years ago   500   400

Living things have developed into a huge range of types through a process called evolution. Evidence of the way living things have evolved is found in fossils dug out of rocks. Fossils show that there have been changes in living things over millions of years.

In addition to these gradual changes there have been a few short periods of sudden change. One of these happened 65 million years ago when the dinosaurs and many other types of animals and plants were wiped out in a very short time.

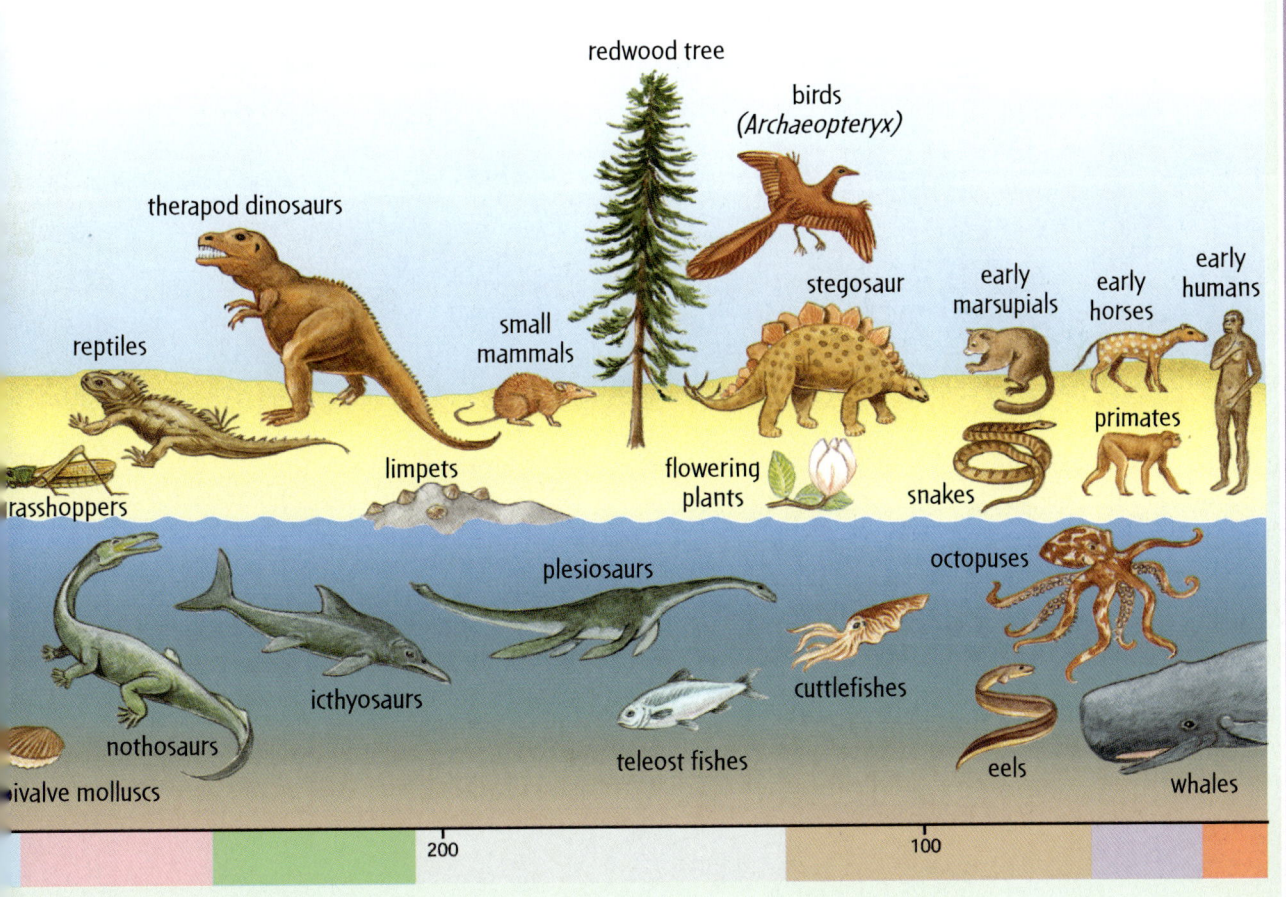

redwood tree

birds
(Archaeopteryx)

therapod dinosaurs

stegosaur

early
marsupials

early
horses

early
humans

small
mammals

reptiles

primates

grasshoppers

limpets

flowering
plants

snakes

plesiosaurs

octopuses

icthyosaurs

cuttlefishes

nothosaurs

teleost fishes

eels

whales

bivalve molluscs

200

100

The Solar System

Our Solar System is made up of the Sun, the nine planets, and their moons. The planets and moons were formed about 4.5 billion years ago at about the same time as the Sun came into being. The inner planets of Mercury, Venus, Earth, and Mars are small and rocky. The outer planets are all, with the exception of Pluto, much larger and made mostly of gas.

Mercury   Venus   Earth   Mars   Jupiter   Saturn   Uranus   Neptune   Pluto

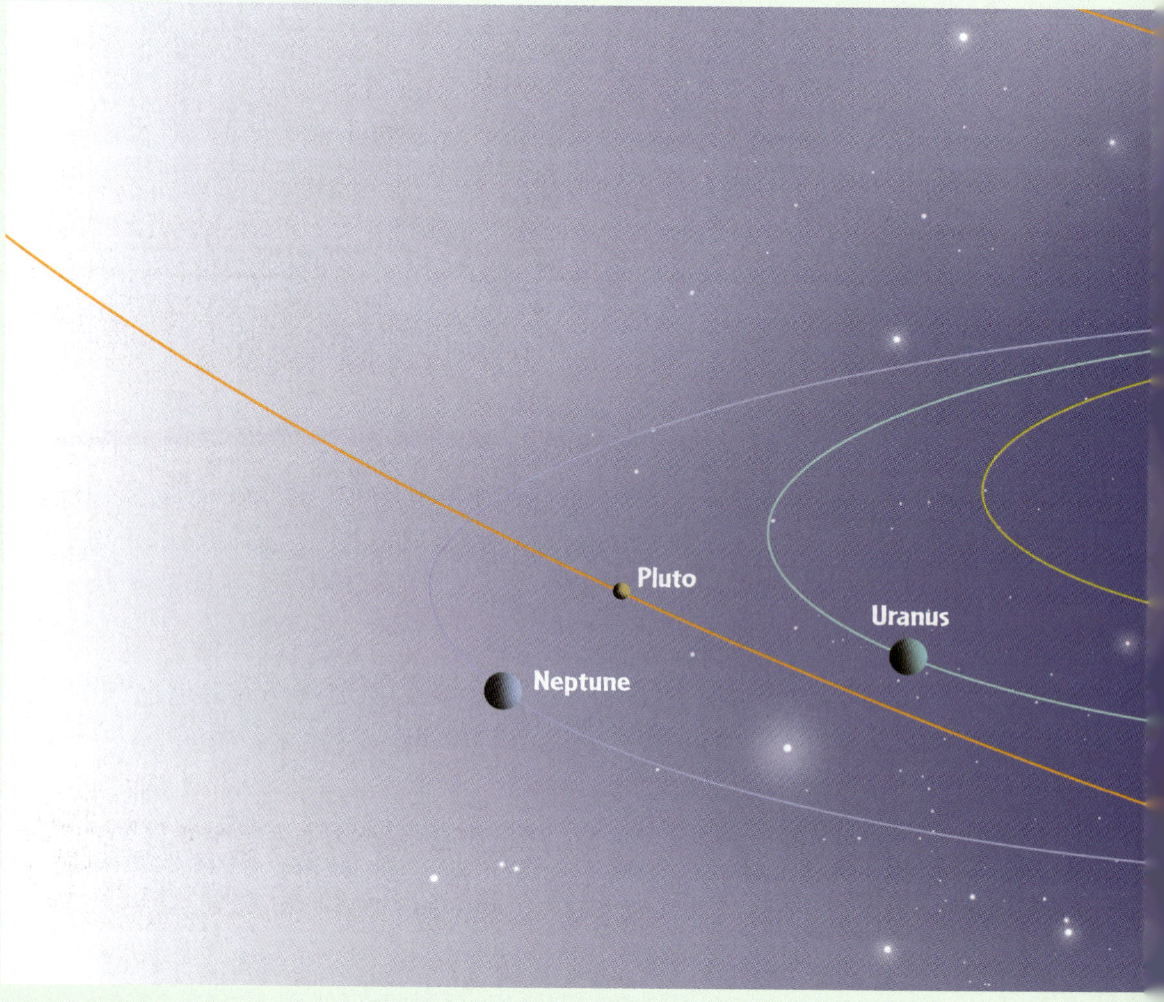

Pluto

Uranus

Neptune

Solar System facts

Planet	Diameter (km)	Number of moons	Average distance from Sun (million km)	Time taken to orbit Sun
Mercury	4878	0	58	88 days
Venus	12104	0	108	225 days
Earth	12756	1	150	365 days
Mars	6976	2	228	687 days
Jupiter	142984	16	778	12 years
Saturn	129660	24	1427	30 years
Uranus	51118	21	2860	84 years
Neptune	49532	8	4500	165 years
Pluto	2360	1	4435 (nearest)	
			7372 (farthest)	248 years

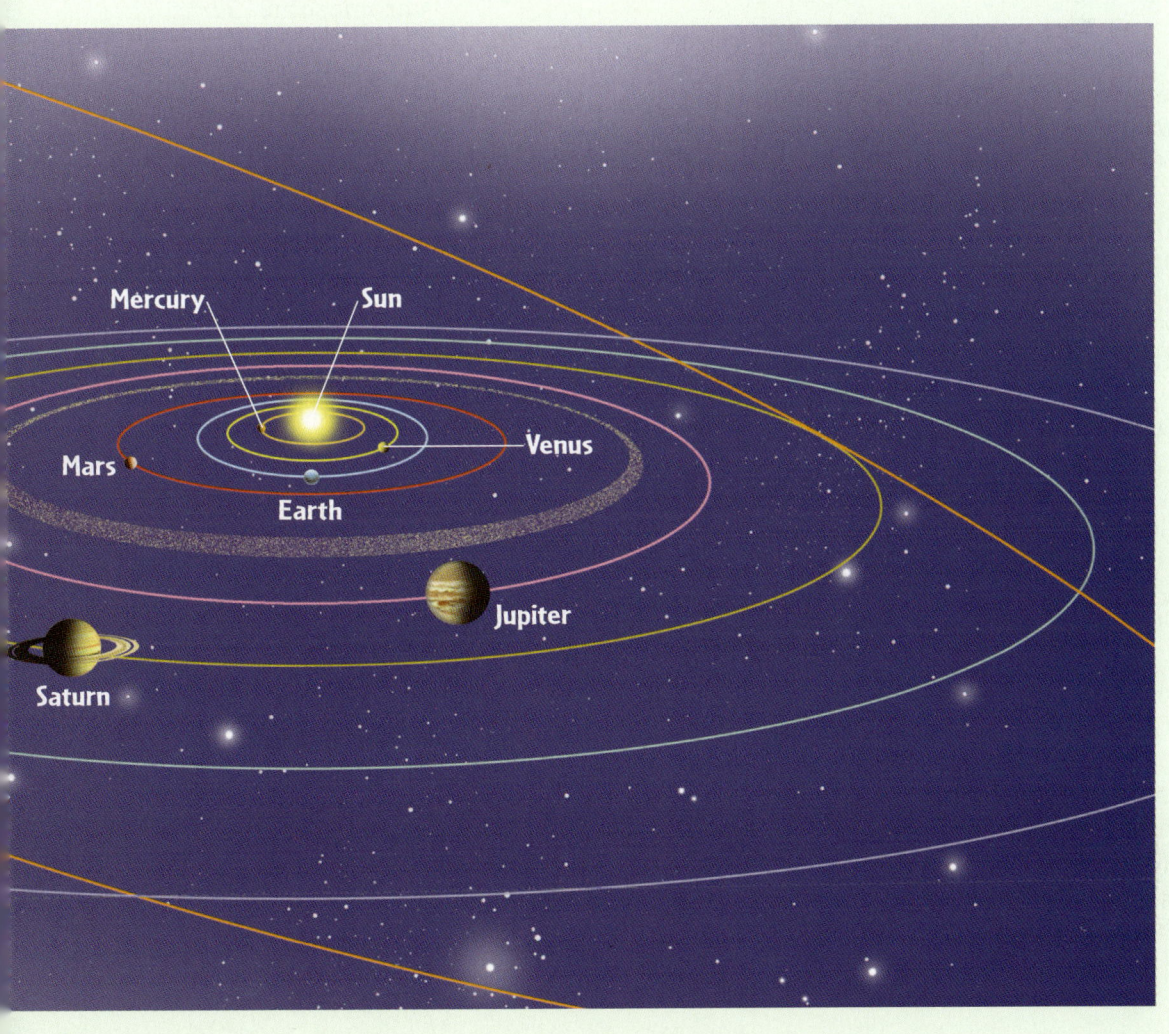

Index